THE KIBBUTZ YAROK EXPERIMENT

A Jewish Summer Camp Experience in
Communal Living

Rabbi Sholom Groesberg, Sc.D., D.H.L.

Copy editor: Henry Grossberg
Photo editor: Allen Singer

Dedicated to my brother, Al, for whom my esteem increases the older we get.

The best remedy for those who are afraid, lonely, or unhappy is to go outside, somewhere where they can be quite alone with the heavens, nature and God. Because only then does one feel that all is as it should be and that God wishes to see people happy, amidst the simple beauty of nature. As long as this exists, and it certainly always will, I know that then there will always be comfort for every sorrow... And I firmly believe that nature brings solace in all troubles. (from the Diary of Anne Frank).

Table of Contents

Foreword by Ruben Arquilevich, Senior Director,
    URJ Camp Newman ·ix
Chapter 1 A Dedicatory Celebration · 1
Chapter 2 The Endowment for Jewish Youth · · · · · · · · · · · · · · · · · 13
Chapter 3 The Camp Newman Story · 41
Chapter 4 The Genesis of Kibbutz Yarok · · · · · · · · · · · · · · · · · · · 53
Chapter 5 The Vision Takes Shape · 65
Chapter 6 Inching Toward Maturity · 77
An Afterword: The Road Ahead for Operation Kibbutz Yarok · · · · · · · · · · 89
Appendix A: A Summary of Permaculture Theory and Practice · · · · · · · · 95
Appendix B: Cosmology, Tikkun Olam, and the Lurianic Scenario · · · · · · 99
Appendix C: An Avodahnik's Essay · 103
A List of Bibliographical References · 105
Index · 107

Foreword

BY RUBEN ARQUILEVICH, SENIOR DIRECTOR, URJ CAMP NEWMAN

*A*t the base of Camp Newman's enchanted forest lies a place called Kibbutz Yarok. In referring to the process of designing and building it, we use the term Operation Kibbutz Yarok (OKY). OKY in our hearts, OKY in our minds, OKY in our souls. What draws us to this fabulous place—to these types of places—in our lives? The natural setting? The peace, quiet, solitude? The various vegetable garden aromas, dirt and mud, baby goats' cries, chicken cackles, budding organic flora? The coyotes, bobcats and raccoons that stroll by? The ospreys, red-tailed hawks, egrets, and blue herons that grace the pond? A Garden of Eden? One's sweat in building mud huts, mud bricks, mud campfire pits? Solar ovens, sustainable kitchens, mud prayer sites? Noshing on fresh-picked blackberries, plums, apples, pears, strawberries, walnuts? Relishing the taste of fresh eggs, just gifted by the chicken that sat in your arms the day before? Cultivating herbs for Havdalah?

Mushroom gardens? The friendship, community, late night camaraderie around the camp fire?

As much as it is about what is created on the land, it is about the experience of living on, and working, the land. No judgment, no production goal; just being, a perpetual Shabbat but with work of the heart and soul and hands and even mind, but not work with the pressure to fulfill an obligation or to please and achieve.

Thank you camp nurse Lisa Katzki, who introduced us to Rabbi Sholom Groesberg, OKY's funder. Rabbi Sholom, in partnership with Camp Newman directors, OKY staffers and avodah campers planted the seeds and nurtured the development of this inspiring vision. The first avodah class ignited the program; all the others since then have carried forward and savored the OKY experience. Kibbutz Yarok now hosts hundreds of children, teens and adults year-round.

I vividly remember visiting my uncle's kibbutz in Israel, at age 10. I remember running naked on the beach as a young child and, along with Uncle Mickey, observing moonlit crabs crawling about on the sand. I remember kibbutz at Camp Swig, and the special experience and destination that it had become. The Jewish environmental and 'back to our roots' movement had its origins millennia ago, and is still alive and well.

Almost a decade has gone by since Ari Vared (today one of Camp Newman's directors) and I took a walk and dreamed about what could transpire on the piece of land where Kibbutz Yarok now stands. These days Joe Glass, an assistant director, and I take that same walk. Most importantly, the kids take that walk, and Rabbi Sholom and his board take that walk—and the vision is unfolding as I write.

Chapter One

A DEDICATORY CELEBRATION

*J*uly 31, 2009, was an auspicious day for our little group. We had assembled on this bright, sunny morning—so typical of Northern California's Bay Area—in the parking lot of Orinda's Safeway supermarket. All accounted for, we set out along Route 24. I, author of this memoiristic chronicle, was one of the passengers in the van. We were breezing along and had gotten, without any difficulty, as far as Route 101 when we hit the traffic jam and now were crawling along. It was a Friday and apparently lots of San Franciscans were intent on getting an early start to the weekend. Fortunately, our driver had logged an untold number of miles in the course of his many years tending to responsibilities as one of his company's real estate managers. Thus, he was intimately acquainted with the region's highways and byways. Unfazed by the traffic snarl, he nonchalantly cut off the freeway and began to negotiate his way through a maze of two-lane roads that honeycomb this rural area. I began to fret: we'll be late for the celebration. Our driver remained silent and simply smiled. Moments later he veered onto a cut-off adorned with a huge banner arching overhead: "Welcome to Camp Newman." We had not only reached our destination, we had arrived on time! I was duly impressed by our driver's dazzling feat of vehicular navigation, and said so. The smile never left his face...

Upon arrival we stopped at the gatehouse. The guard on duty asked about the purpose of the visit. I explained that we were members of an organization that helps fund Kibbutz Yarok's operations, and had been invited to participate in a dedication ceremony. He nodded OK, and then scanned his visitors list. There was no mention of one of our passengers. We were told to pull inside the gate and park over on the side. Someone would be down to identify us. Frankly, I was impressed by the tight security, but some in our group were rather vexed by the delay because other cars were pulling up and passing through. I calmed things down a bit by pointing out that this was Shabbat and parents were coming up for the weekend. Shortly, a staff member who had driven down to the gate in a go-cart verified that the unidentified visitor was OK. Cleared for entry, our van followed the go-cart up to Newman's dining hall. There to greet us was a small welcoming committee. The camp's executive director, Ruben Arquilevich, had been joined by Ari Vared, his assistant director; by Dena Kaufman, the camp's development director; and by Lisa Katzki, the camp's head nurse.

Kibbutz Yarok started up in 2009 as an experimental project initiated and supervised by Camp Newman. Designed to be a self-contained, self-sustainable, and eco-friendly cooperative community, it was being built during Newman's summer session by teenage campers who volunteered for the assignment. Newman's long-range objective was the creation of a year-round community able to provide guests, of any age, with a vicarious experience of life on an Israeli kibbutz.

Two of the passengers in the van, the driver Allen Singer and myself, are board members of a California Nonprofit Public Benefit Corporation established in 1999. Named the Endowment for Jewish Youth, the Corporation, pursuant to its stated mission, supports Kibbutz Yarok financially with an annual grant of $20,000. Allen and I were in Camp Newman on that day for the primary purpose of viewing first-hand, midway through the summer session, the accomplishments chalked up thus far by the nascent kibbutz. Secondarily, we were present in order to participate in a dedicatory ceremony, and also in order to experience Shabbat as observed at Camp Newman.

So here we were, being greeted by the welcoming committee, and Lisa Katzki is *kvelling* (a Yiddishism for 'silently bursting with pride'). She's not only a member of our board, but she also brokered the kibbutz deal; and moreover, she came up with the fledgling community's name: Kibbutz Yarok (*yarok* is Hebrew for the color 'green'). Following the preliminary exchange of pleasantries, we embarked on the program our hosts had arranged for us. It began with a visit to the kibbutz site. By this time we had been joined by a few latecomers: Lisa's spouse, Dan; Allen's friend, Shelley; and Amanda Pazornik, a reporter from *jweekly*: the Bay Area's local Jewish weekly. She's here to cover the event. So, all of us caravanned up to the kibbutz site, along a rutted one-lane dirt road that's undoubtedly a quagmire after a rain. But today the skies were cerulean blue and not a wisp of cloud was in sight.

The 20-acre site had been allocated to the kibbutz by Camp Newman's Board of Directors. It represented a small parcel of the 400+ acres comprising the camp's property. The site was a secluded space, a 20-minute walk from the main camp. We saw a plateau-like area completely surrounded by awe-inspiring mountains visible in the distance. A small but quite lovely pond reposed placidly nearby. All in all, it was a magnificent setting for a kibbutz. Some teenagers, attending to various chores on the site, stopped working to observe the goings-on. The first object that caught our eye was a strange nondescript structure: four walls, seemingly made of mud, forming a rectangular enclosure without a top. Ruben, aware of the general puzzlement, explained that was the rudiment of the first bunkhouse in which future kibbutzniks would be living.

Next, we ambled over to something resembling a dilapidated barn. Ruben informed us that this was the embryonic predecessor of a future live animal farm. At this time its inhabitants consisted of a mule, a goat, and some chickens—who were totally oblivious to city people gawking at them. Next he led us to what was clearly a thriving vegetable garden.

The corn plants were six feet tall. Ruben pointed out that this organic garden had already yielded—we were not even into August yet—a bumper crop of eggplants, zucchini squash, tomatoes, pea-pods, and corn. He picked up, and displayed for our edification, a monstrous zucchini the size—no exaggeration—of a little league baseball bat. He remarked, with justifiable pride, that the yielded produce is always incorporated into Camp Newman's Shabbat dinners. Moreover, he mentioned that all the work associated with producing the vegetable crop—tilling, sowing, weeding, irrigating, harvesting—had been done by avodahniks.

Some in our little troop of visitors had never heard this word before, but only the reporter was willing to risk displaying her ignorance. She asked about it. Ruben—ever the consummate diplomat—commended her for the question and then explained that the name derives from the Hebrew word *avodah*, which carries the dual meaning of 'work' and 'service'. Avodahniks are teenage campers who voluntarily commit to working on projects in support of Camp Newman's general operational needs, of which Kibbutz Yarok is one of many. The brief tour completed, and just a wee bit weary by now, we trudged up to a cleared space. Lo and Behold! Perhaps as many as a hundred or so avodahniks and staff people were ranged in a large circle, waiting for Ruben and the visitors to return from their tour. It was an electrifying moment and our weariness vanished in a flash. We found places within the encircling ring, linked arms with the neighbor on each side, and the dedication ceremony commenced.

Ruben offered some welcoming remarks, introduced the guests, and publicly thanked the many avodahniks who had worked diligently, often from sun-up to sun-down, at laying the physical foundation of Kibbutz Yarok. They had cleared the land, repaired the animal farm's sagging fences, built benches from pieces of scrap lumber lying around, and with their own hands constructed the as-yet unfinished initial archetype of Kibbutz Yarok's future bunkhouses. We, the visitors, were unable to desist from acknowledging their accomplishment; we applauded them.

Then, two younger staffers playing guitars led the entire assemblage in a pair of songs. There followed four readings, each written and read aloud by someone who stepped forward from the circle. Lastly, after displaying it for all to see, an avodahnik read aloud a four-page epistolary document hand written on yellow craft paper. The cover page consisted of a drawing depicting mountains and clouds in the background, while in the foreground could be seen a tree and a canoe among rushes. The cover page carried the title OPERATION KIBBUTZ YAROK in large letters. The first inside page contained the following text:

> On behalf of the Avodahniks class of 2009, we would all like to say a huge thank you for all the incredible mitzvot you have done for us. This is surely the best Avodah project Camp Newman has seen. Thank you so much for this opportunity to exercise Tikkun Olam at the place we call home. You have presented us, and future campers in Avodah, with a fantastic chance to change the face of camp for the better; to make it a more eco-friendly environment. We are so lucky to be giving future campers the gift of an unforgettable experience, as if they were living on a kibbutz in Israel. Every day we go to OKY, we learn more about each other and how to work with one another, leadership, hard work, and dedication. We owe the project of our lives to you! Thank you!

The third page of the document was headed, in large-sized Hebrew letters, by the two words *TODAH RABBAH* (Hebrew for 'thank you so much'). Underneath was a sub-heading: The Avodah Class of 2009. The remainder of the page was covered with signatures.

The formal part of the dedication ceremony concluded with the traditional ritual of affixing a *mezuzah* to the doorway of a Jewish dwelling. The dwelling in the present instance was the mud structure intended to become Yarok's first bunkhouse. Having had a chance to look at the hut more closely, my engineering background enabled me to appreciate that what the structure lacked in esthetic beauty was compensated by the cleverness of its utilitarian design. The mud-impregnated thick walls would make for excellent insulators against the vagaries of California weather. The rectangular openings high up on the walls would admit light and permit fresh air to circulate, thus obviating the need for windows. The thickness of the walls, roughly ten inches as I eyeballed them, would ensure that the sun's rays wouldn't directly enter the structure's interior during hot weather, thus obviating the need for air conditioning.

In order to witness the ritual of affixing the mezuzah, about 30 or so people were able to crowd into the as-yet unroofed hut; the rest remained outside. The ritual would be performed by Rabbi Jason Gwasdoff of Temple Israel in Stockton, CA. Each summer Camp Newman brings on-site ten or so ordained Reform rabbis who voluntarily serve as spiritual leaders for a period of two weeks. Each is assigned a cohort of campers comprising his or her charges. Appropriately, Rabbi Gwasdoff had been honored with the privilege of performing the ritual because the wards assigned to him on his 'watch' were all avodahniks.

As a prelude to affixing the mezuzah, he established a perspective for the entire ritual by pinpointing its special significance on this occasion: "Just by putting our hands into mud and onto these walls, this beautiful house teaches us so much about sustainability and protecting the earth." He then linked present practice to ancient tradition. He held up the mezuzah in a slanted position for all to see, and recounted the story of how back in the Middle Ages two prominent rabbinical sages differed regarding the proper positioning of the mezuzah. One insisted on the vertical, the other on the horizontal. The issue was resolved through compromise: a slanted position. This important lesson regarding compromise, the rabbi pointed out, characterizes Jewish life throughout its venerable history. Hopefully, the spirit of compromise will continue to inform future relationships in Jewish life. He concluded by reciting the requisite blessing, then affixing the mezuzah, and finally leading everyone in the traditional *Shehecheyanu*—a prayer recited upon every important occasion in the life of an individual or a community.

Ruben asked me if I would like to say something. Never one to decline an opportunity to speechify before any audience numbering more than three persons, I launched into my oration by thanking Ruben, the staff, and the avodahniks for what had been accomplished and for the inspiring experience it would prove to be for future campers. I concluded my remarks by pointing out that Operation Kibbutz Yarok represented a concise and accurate overview of my entire vocational life. It combined my first career in engineering with my second career in the rabbinate. I closed with: "I shall cherish OKY forever." Silence followed. But I was neither disappointed nor disconcerted, because it was an unembellished avowal of a truth.

The dedication ceremony concluded with the obligatory group photo. Allen, our spiffy chauffeur, also happens to be a skillful photographer. He always manages to have somewhere on his person a camera at the ready. Following the group photo, people were informally milling about. To my surprise, and undiluted pleasure, individual avodahniks approached me and asked me to pose for a photo while a friend took a snapshot. As if this weren't enough, some of the female variety *gave me a hug.* My comparatively fragile ego went soaring sky high, but I was quickly brought down to reality; people in our little entourage were mouthing murmurings about lunch. Lisa recommended lunch at Checkers Restaurant, an eatery she'd visited many times. It's located 15 minutes away in charming Calistoga, a popular tourist attraction nestled in Napa Valley's wine country. So we headed there.

The place is tidy, the waitresses nimble, the menu extensive, the portions ample—all to our complete satisfaction. Having finished lunch, Lisa announced—to my total surprise—that I'm picking up the check. Tumultuous applause followed, so how could I decline the honor… We returned to camp; amiable conviviality reigned. Thus far it had been a busy and tiring day, but also exhilarating and emotionally draining. Lisa, in her customary considerateness, had set aside a quiet room for me in the camp infirmary. I was grateful for the opportunity to take a bit of a rest before the Sabbath would begin.

—⁑—

The purple dusk of twilight was stealing across the meadows of Camp Newman's landscape. A sudden stillness enveloped a space that just moments before had been all hustle and bustle. Everyone in camp —campers, staffers, guests, parents visiting for the day—was preparing for Shabbat; each in his or her own way. And now they sallied forth, all streaming toward the camp's outdoor prayer site: A huge amphitheater set into a hillside among stands of majestic trees. Tiers of wooden benches arranged in semicircles were gradually filling up with campers. They ranged in age from second graders to high schoolers. Dressed in white, they were symbolically preparing to greet the Sabbath Queen.

On the spacious stage up front, staffers and avodahniks were busily engaged in checking out the sound system, tuning musical instruments, coordinating with vocal soloists. The entire amphitheater was alive with noisy chatter among neighbors, and needless to say, ubiquitous picture-taking. There was also a fair amount of restless craning-about in order to check on who's sitting next to whom. Ruben stepped up to the microphone at center stage. This simple move sent a tacit message to the audience. The assemblage of high-spirited, ebullient, jabbering campers magically grew silent. After an appropriate pause, Ruben welcomed everyone—parents, guests, faculty, staff, and campers. Without further ado, the musicians and singers on stage burst forth with a medley of songs. The campers knew all the melodies and the words, and full-throated harmonies pierced the heavens. If the Holy *Shechinah* ('divine Presence') is somewhere up there, listening, she has surely descended upon this place and spread her canopy of peace upon it.

The Shabbat service commenced with the traditional lighting of the candles and the blessing over the wine. On this occasion Ruben had chosen to bestow an honor on all the visiting rabbis ('the faculty'), and also on our visiting group of board members. He invited them to come up to the stage and join in the rituals. Lisa and Dan Katzki went up, as did Allen Singer and Shelley Ruhman. I elected to stay put. I was comfortably settled in the uppermost row because there was a wall to lean back against, and because my perch afforded a panoramic view of the proceedings on stage. Besides, I didn't feel like undertaking what was for me an arduous trip down to the stage and back.

The worship service continued with the customary portions as laid out in the prayer book. However, I noted that many passages were generously 'enhanced' with musical offerings, imaginative interpretations, homegrown skits, and a sprinkling of low-level clowning. Then the evening's guest performer sauntered on stage, to much acclamation. I asked the youngster on my right who this is, and learned he's Rick Recht, a popular performer at Jewish youth gatherings throughout the United States. Guitar in hand, he led the audience in song after song. As an encore he honored a few requests shouted out by the audience.

The service concluded with closing remarks by Ruben, followed by an interesting recessional. The camp counselors formed a double row at the exit of the prayer site, creating an honor guard for the departing campers. Then, one after another, a group of campers accompanied by a guitar-playing song leader filed out of the amphitheater in orderly fashion and headed for the dining hall.

Inside the brightly lit dining hall each cohort of campers, accompanied by its counselor, sat together at pre-assigned tables. The medical staff, the faculty members, and our group randomly found seats at a group of specially designated tables. My neighboring fellow diners were affable and the conversation was engaging. A member of the nursing staff was seated across the table from me. We'd been chatting during the meal and then something occurred that piqued my curiosity. On my right, four tables had been set up near the wall. Sitting atop each was a corrugated cardboard box bearing a placard with some writing too small for me to read. Behind each table a camp nurse stood. Suddenly, bunches of campers came up to the tables and sorted themselves into queues, one before each table. Puzzled by this, I asked my chat friend about it.

"What are these campers doing lined up at those tables?"

"It's meds time." I nodded in understanding. She was referring to prescribed medications that must be taken by the youngsters wherever they may be.

"But why so many?"

"Special circumstances. The Swine Flu has been circulating, and we've been extra cautious. In fact, we delayed camp opening for two weeks so that we could be fully prepared for all contingencies."

"An ounce of prevention..."

"Exactly."

"Back when I was a camper, many decades ago, I don't remember anything remotely resembling this."

"Welcome to the S-generation. S is for sedentary."

The meds routine completed, the Shabbat dinner got under way. The waiters, in an intriguing turnabout, are senior camp staffers, headed by Ari Vared, the assistant camp director. This turn-about conveys an important lesson that, I have no doubt, is not lost upon these youngsters. The waiters are bustling about: sure-handed, quick, and efficient. The food, served family style, is plentiful, with seconds gladly forthcoming for the asking. Alcoholic beverages are prohibited by local ordinances, so we make do with fruit juice and lemon-flavored water. As for the food itself, one would hardly classify it as commissary cooking. To me, famished as I am, the menu encroaches upon territory reserved for haute cuisine. The appetizer course, already set out on the tables, consists of salad, pita, hummus, challah, and an eggplant casserole. (The casserole is delicious; and the eggplant, I am informed, has been grown in Kibbutz Yarok's organic vegetable garden.) The main course is herbed chicken and rice. Brownies, a specialty of the house and a universal favorite, close out the delectable meal.

Dinner over, the room is a riot of songs, and cheers, and adolescent hi-jinks. Then comes what for me is the highlight of the entire Shabbat meal experience. The dining hall resounds with an exuberant chanting of the *birkat ha-mazon,* the traditional blessing that expresses gratitude for nourishment. My heart is gladdened as I witness this multitude of young Jewish boys and girls joyously intoning these hallowed words and melodies; because this seemingly inconsequential affirmation of Jewish identity will contribute, in ways yet unseen, to the perpetuation of the Jewish peoplehood.

Although dinner is over, the Shabbat festivities are far from over. Everyone streams up to the floodlit basketball court. A potpourri of songs and Israeli folk dance music blasts forth from an industrial-strength loudspeaker system. The leaders are leading, and the energized crowd of campers is singing, shouting, gyrating, whooping. As for me, I don't recognize even a fraction of what's going on. Until, that is, I suddenly hear the music for the Israeli folk dance *HaRo'ah HaK'tanah.* Dancers go whirling 'round in a circle, and I'm transported back to my youthful days. The spirit is all too willing, but the flesh, alas, is all too weak...

The frantic festivities will be ending at curfew time. Regrettably, our group is obliged to depart for home before then because we've got an hour and a half of Friday night traffic to contend with. But Allen, our talented navigator, confidently assures us: "Not to worry." And once again, he's right. He negotiates all the twists and turns flawlessly, with nary a moment's indecision. He's not even perturbed by the closure of an approach to the Carquinez Bridge that leads into Contra Costa County. He deftly weaves through back ways which are totally unfamiliar to the rest of us. And *voilà!* We're back on the bridge and home is minutes away.

It's already 11 o'clock, and it's been a long day. I'm tired, but happy. July 31, 2009, has been a memorable day for me. I've been privileged to witness the initiation of a process whereby a cherished vision is becoming manifest as an embryonic, but physically palpable, kibbutz. Kudos to Ruben Arquilevich and all his associates.

Chapter Two

THE ENDOWMENT FOR
JEWISH YOUTH

*I*t was only later in life, at age 60, that I decided upon a second career in the rabbinate. In fact, there was very little in my earlier years to suggest that I might have any inclination to such a career choice. On the contrary, although I grew up in a thoroughly Jewish cultural environment, there was very little that connoted any predilection for engaging in acts of religious observance.

My immigrant parents left their respective countries of origin— my father: Poland; my mother: Palestine—in order to escape from religiously observant homes that were insufferably suffocating. They separately made their way to New York, and seeking the comfort of a Yiddish-speaking community (their native tongue) each happened to join the same branch of *Poalei Tziyon* (Hebrew for 'Workers of Zion'). It was a movement founded in the early 1900s whose ideology combined Marxist theory with Jewish nationalistic aspirations. In brief: my future parents met; fell in love; got married; and raised a family of three sons, of which I'm the middle son.

I grew up in Brighton Beach, a neighborhood in Brooklyn, NY, so thoroughly Jewish that the public school I attended, P.S. 100 on West First Street, closed down on all our major holidays. My home environment was culturally Jewish, but non-observant in terms of religious practice. For example, on Friday evening my mother kindled Shabbat candles, recited the blessings, and served a traditional meal. However, this was more a manifestation of cultural allegiance than religious persuasion.

There was nothing particularly Jewish about my childhood years. However, in my high school years I joined a local chapter of a fraternal organization for Jewish teenage boys named AZA. At that time I was into team sports and my chapter belonged to a league that featured inter-chapter play. After graduation my thoughts turned to college, but this was something my family could ill afford. But there did exist the City College of New York—a totally tuition-free school for New York high schoolers whose grade-point-average qualified them for admission. Fortunately, I made the cut and chose to major in engineering.

Upon graduating, I was chagrined to discover that I was unable to find an engineering job. There were openings, but not for Jews—cultural, religious, atheistic, secular, or otherwise. The door was closed to me. Then World War II erupted in Europe and America's Lend-Lease program got under way. The Brooklyn Navy Yard began to retrofit ships for wartime convoy duty and the Yard found it necessary to subcontract some of the work to a company that manufactured type-setting machines. The company was now obliged to cope with its own shortage of engineering talent, of which I was apparently an acceptable specimen. I was hired, and this was the beginning of a lengthy career in my chosen profession.

After eight years of professional practice, I moved into academe, joining the faculty first at Stevens Institute of Technology (Hoboken, NJ); thence, offered a promotion, at Widener University (Chester, PA). Once there, I moved up through the hierarchy of professorial ranks, a process that culminated in my appointment as Dean of Engineering.

The years went rolling by and I was contentedly ensconced in my commodious office, seated in my padded leather swivel chair, and idly musing—when it dawned on me that the zest I used to bring to my vocational activities had seeped away. I had made the most of what my talent and skills permitted in a satisfying engineering career, and there was nothing further for me along that road. I'd made all the stops; been there and done that, so to speak. In 1980, I resigned my deanship at Widener, declined an invitation to stay on as a tenured professor, donated my library to the university, and simply left; without the faintest idea of what to do next. I still had some gas left in my tank, whereupon I took to thinking about the possibility of undertaking something entirely new in my life. How about a second career? My first career had been interesting, remunerative, and fulfilling. But I'd chosen it for material reasons. Now, however, I wanted something that had a spiritual dimension—something that spoke to my heart.

I was now face to face with a fundamental existential question: What was really important to me at this stage in my life? Reviewing various alternatives, I analyzed each, and one by one discarded them—except for one that refused to be dismissed. Rooted somewhere in the substrate of my very being was my Jewish identity. Apparently, the cultural milieu of my childhood had left an imprint on my subliminal apparatus. But how could I transform this nebulous aspiration of doing something Jewish into a tangible course of action? Given the many factors in play—age, experience, aptitude, temperament—two possibilities seemed to be practicable. Either move laterally into teaching Jewish Studies somewhere in academe, or start anew and strike for the rabbinate. I'd done enough teaching in my lifetime—time to try something really different. I chose the latter.

As I had been forewarned, I could not expect much of a career in the rabbinate unless I obtained ordination from a chartered seminary. Accordingly, I diligently made the rounds of inquiry and interviews, but to no avail. However, the Academy for Jewish Religion turned things around for me. Ordained in 1984, credential in hand and bursting with enthusiasm, I embarked upon my second career.

I dispatched a slew of resumés in all directions. Only one offer eventually materialized. I accepted it and off I went to a small start-up congregation in that prestigious center of Jewish life and learning called Plano, TX. I served in that pulpit for three years; enough to give the congregation some direction, and to develop a lay leadership capable of nurturing the fledgling enterprise. I subsequently served start-ups in Irving, TX, and Antioch, CA. In 1997, I retired from the active pulpit. Time to take it easy.

I relocated to a retirement community in Walnut Creek, CA, and settled comfortably into a small but adequate condominium. But still harboring a desire to keep my hand in, so to speak, I organized a local 'congregation without walls' (Congregation Shir Neshamah), serving as their spiritual leader on a volunteer basis. Life was good. However, a disturbing thought began gnawing at my equanimity. I was living in a retirement community; no one under 55 allowed. Seeing so many older folks around, many in disrepair, was a daily disquieting reminder that every passing day brought me closer to my own mortality. I decided it was time to put my earthly affairs in order. Time to do some estate planning.

On recommendation of a friend I engaged the services of an estate planning attorney. We arranged for an appointment. After introducing ourselves, I described what I was seeking, and inquired about his fee. For uncomplicated estate work, as this appears to be, he charges a flat fee: half down, the balance on completion. Given the long string of unhappy experiences I've scuffled through with assorted exemplars of the legal profession, I decide on the spot: this is my guy! (Besides, I note from a framed diploma on the wall, his degree is from Harvard Law.)

Our first order of business would be the writing of my will. I'd already told him about my major bequests; however, he pointed out, I'd said nothing about the disposition of my residual estate. No, I had not. This was indeed a matter that required careful consideration. I had to decide about disposal of my estate to a beneficiary about whose activities, after my demise, I would have absolutely no knowledge or control. The best I could do, while still animate and sentient, was create some sort of entity that would carry forward, in the *here and now*, an activity which reflected (in my imagination) what I would like to do after I departed this life. To put it another way, I would try to fashion a prototype of the future, while living in the present. The future is now, so to speak.

So far, so good. Now I faced the specific question: What kind of entity? As a rabbi, I firmly believed that my fundamental and over-riding obligation was to contribute to the well-being of the Jewish peoplehood, and to help, in some miniscule way, ensure its survival. If such were the basic objective, then the target of my efforts ought to be Jewish boys and girls who collectively become the peoplehood's succeeding generation. Hence, the matter is settled: I shall earmark those assets for some sort of activity that serves to strengthen the sense of self-identity and group-identity among Jewish youth.

This important issue having been resolved, I thought it prudent to form a 'kitchen cabinet' to assist me in my decision-making. Whereupon I assembled a group of hand-picked individuals, each of whom I genuinely liked and had known for at least a decade. I respected their ability to make sound judgments in matters of consequence. I was impressed by their past and present vocational achievements. Finally, I admired their willingness to serve voluntarily as members of my advisory committee. So we got to work.

After lengthy, yet elucidative, discussions we decided to establish a charitable non-profit corporation. This would enable us to acquire tax-exempt status, and also make it easier to obtain protection against personal liability. In 1999, a California Nonprofit Public Benefit Corporation came into being. Adorned with a name suggested by Lisa Katzki, a member of our advisory committee, the Endowment for Jewish Youth (EJY) was born. The Articles of Incorporation included a mandatory set of Bylaws. Among these was a statement describing the mission to which the Endowment for Jewish Youth devoted itself. It reads as follows:

> Continuity of the Jewish people is assured only if each succeeding generation commits itself to Judaism's value system and its cultural traditions. The purpose of the Corporation shall be to contribute to this endeavor by supporting, through financial subsidy, activities whose purpose is to foster a positive self-image among Jewish youth and to strengthen their sense of Jewish identity.

The members of the erstwhile advisory committee became charter members of the Corporation's Board of Directors. With the organizational framework in place, we turned our attention to formulating and implementing a suitable program for EJY. Given our stated mission, the issue was how to bring Jewish young people closer to their cultural heritage, and how to strengthen their sense of Jewish identity. Investigation revealed that, on the basis of broad consensus, there were three proven modalities for accomplishing this: I. Enrollment in a Jewish day school; II. Participation in the program called Birthright Israel; and III. A stay at a Jewish summer sleep-away camp.

I. A Jewish day school meets full-time, and provides both a Jewish and a secular education in one facility. They became popular in the mid 1950s among parents dissatisfied with either the old-fashioned talmud torahs, or the extant urban public schools. The Jewish day school movement was flourishing: A 2009 survey revealed that 802 Jewish day schools enroll roughly 228,000 children from 1st through 12th grades. However, the board eliminated this option because youngsters enrolled in a Jewish day school were hardly likely to be seriously deficient in their sense of Jewish identity.

II. Birthright Israel sponsors free 10-day trips to Israel for Jewish young men and women. The purpose is to foster an acquaintance with, and an appreciation of, their cultural heritage. The sponsor pays for round-trip airfare, lodging, meals, transportation, and touring within Israel. Nearly a quarter million individuals have participated in the program since 2000. However, the board dismissed this program as an option because only persons between the ages of 18 and 26 were eligible. Hence, Birthright Israel participants were too old for the cohort we had in mind. That left the third option.

III. EJY went about exploring this option by first contacting The Foundation for Jewish Camp. This non-profit seeks to advance the well-being of Jewish sleep-away camps in North America. It makes its array of programs available to more than 170 quality Jewish camps accommo-dating some 70,000 campers and their 10,000 counselors. The organiza-tion assured us that what EJY had in mind would certainly contribute to the effort of helping 'turn Jewish youth into spirited and engaged Jewish adults'. We decided to explore this option further.

Poking around on the internet, we learned of a comprehensive study that sought to determine the impact of a Jewish sleep-away camp experi-ence on one's subsequent adult life. The study consolidated the findings of close to 25 surveys sponsored by local Jewish communities, ranging geographically from Atlanta to Seattle. These surveys were conducted between 2000 and 2008. The study's research team first established four activities as being indicative of a commitment to a Jewish way of life: I. Donation to a Jewish charity; II. Lighting Shabbat candles; III. Synagogue attendance; and IV. Emotional attachment to Israel. The raw data to be processed consisted of responses given by participants in the various surveys belonging to either of two categories: those who had, and those who had not, attended a Jewish sleep-away summer camp. From this accumulated data, the researchers arrived at their statistically significant results. In all four of the above-mentioned activities campers registered a higher likelihood of participation than did the non-campers: I. Charity donation: 30% higher; II. Shabbat candles: 37% higher; III. Synagogue attendance: 45% higher; IV. Emotional attachment to Israel: 55% higher.

On the strength of these findings, and after factoring in such rel-evant data as were supplied by the Foundation for Jewish Camp, EJY decided on a modus operandi for carrying out its mission. We would award scholarships to help defray the cost of an otherwise unaffordable stay at any quality Jewish summer sleep-away camp in the United States or Canada. Such a program lay within EJY's mandate, and was compatible with our modest resources of time and money.

After a few years of experimentation we had fixed upon an acceptable plan of performance. We would conduct our business entirely by means of email, a website designed and managed by board member Michael Cohen, and a rented post office box. In order to publicize our program we relied on social service agencies, Jewish camps, and word-of-mouth communication. Applications for scholarships could be obtained solely by download from our website. We next turned our attention to the application form. Inasmuch as board members had agreed to voluntarily process them, we wished to keep the application easy to peruse and short in length: four pages to fit a standard 11x17 sheet of paper. The application would include pro forma stuff and questions designed to elicit information for determining the financial circumstances of the household. Concerning the latter, the question arose regarding whether or not to request information involving financial disclosure (in the world of philanthropy known as 'means testing').

We knew that philanthropic organizations involved in eleemosynary giving made means testing standard operating practice. Should EJY be contrarian? It would certainly reduce the burden on our volunteer application processors. On the other hand, it would increase the likelihood that malefactors, with no deterrent other than conscience, would victimize EJY. Ultimately, the board agreed that such occasional monetary losses were counterbalanced by lessened demands in time and effort on the part of the processors. Besides, by not asking people to publicly undress themselves financially, EJY surely entitled itself to an ethical check-mark…

So we commenced operations as per plan. Applications were downloaded, filled out, and mailed in to our post office box. Our volunteer processors sifted through the applications and winnowed out those deemed less worthy of the $300 scholarship we awarded. They then carefully evaluated the remaining applications and separated out the twenty-five awardees; the number specified in accordance with budgetary constraints. Finally, letters of regret were sent to all applicants who had failed to make the cut. Also, letters of acceptance were sent to the awardees, and a check was sent to the camp that had been chosen by the applicant.

Year after year, EJY continued to do business as usual, despite now and then learning by chance that so-and-so had taken advantage of EJY's gullibility. But we consoled ourselves with the thought that somehow, somewhere, we were doing a bit of good. Thus, we annually awarded— without any quality control system in place—twenty-five $300 scholarships. Things continued in this fashion until the year 2008. In that year an unanticipated development led to an incredible sea change in EJY's modus operandi.

I was at home, listlessly moping around and brooding over the less than satisfactory state of affairs at the Endowment for Jewish Youth— the creature I had midwifed. Then the phone rang and jostled me out of my funk. It was board member Lisa Katzki, that summer working as the lead nurse at Camp Newman. She excitedly told me about an off-duty chat she'd just had with camp director Ruben Arquilevich (whom she's known for 14 years). He mentioned something about a new project he's trying to get off the ground. He wished to establish, as an adjunct to Newman, an experimental camp community occupying its own site. It would be a self-sustaining, eco-friendly, cooperative mini-camp modeled after, and sharing the values of, an Israeli kibbutz. Moreover, it would be built, operated, and inhabited by campers.

Lisa paused momentarily so that I could digest this news. But I could intuit what she had in mind. I said nothing and she continued. Newman's board has given its approval of the project and is agreeable to lending ancillary assistance. However, Ruben is responsible for finding a portion of the necessary financial support. She paused once again, and it did not take me very long to determine my position. I really like this project. I *really* like it. Although EJY's participation would still amount to check-writing, there was an element of direct involvement. Camp Newman, in Santa Rosa, is sufficiently close so that we'd be able to make on-site visits periodically. We could therefore see, first-hand, tangible evidence of progress (or lack thereof). Moreover, this project brought together my two careers: engineering and the rabbinate. I suggested to Lisa that she inform Ruben of EJY's interest, and invite him to submit to our board a proposal providing the essential details.

He complied with the request. Newman's board has marked off the 20 acres that will serve as the kibbutz site. Supervised by Newman personnel, teenagers who volunteer for the assignment will design, construct, and operate the kibbutz. Financially, Ruben estimates that the project will require additional support on the order of $20,000 per annum. Included in the request was a projected three-year plan of performance.

EJY's board met, liked the idea, but wanted to know (as did I) if I could manage this fiscally. I discussed the matter with both my financial advisor and my tax consultant. They considered it feasible, provided I was willing to annually draw down the necessary sum from my estate, all the while protecting a reserve sufficient to meet possible health contingencies. I went back to the board and reported that, barring catastrophic illness, I'd been assured that the proposed annual 20k grant was feasible. Thus, reassured, the board voted unanimously to proceed by asking Ruben to submit for its consideration a proposed plan of performance. After studying the plan, the board drew up a Memorandum of Understanding for Ruben's approval. Once some details were jointly ironed out, I, as president of EJY, and Ruben, as executive director of Camp Newman (sponsor of Kibbutz Yarok), signed the document. As of May 28, 2009, the partnership was official.

Since then, under the watchful eye of EJY board member Lillian Roselin (who works professionally as a grants administrator), things moved ahead satisfactorily; EJY renewed its annual grant and Camp Newman sent us its annual report. In fact, there was nothing much for us to do, other than sign the check. Perhaps it was time to dissolve EJY; I could forward the annual 20k grant directly to Newman. Accordingly, the board met on September 21, 2011; briefly discussed the issue; and unanimously voted to dissolve. As the year came to a close, EJY was no longer in existence. But no tears were shed. It had been a gladsome experience for all those involved in managing its affairs. Needless to say, without the board's inestimable assistance none of our achievements would have been possible. Out of sincere gratitude, I find it necessary to list by name, in alphabetical order, all those who—at some point in its history—voluntarily served on the board, thereby contributing to the transformation of a mission statement into a functional institution—the Endowment for Jewish Youth—that incontestably did tangible good.

—ɷ—

• Martin Abrams, Ph.D. (engineering), Purdue University; Numerical simulation of physical phenomena. (ret.)
• Michael M. Cohen, O.D. (optometry), Pacific University; Consultant to the ophthalmological industry.
• Henry Grossberg, J.D. (law), Case Western Reserve University; Administrator for non-profit institutions.
• Lisa Katzki, B.S. (nursing), California State University, Hayward; Principal in a first aid & emergency supply business.
• Cheryl Lebow, J.D. (law), University of California, Hastings; Staff attorney for county-mandated child support programs.
• Lillian Roselin, M.S. (rehab counseling), San Francisco State University; Health foundation's program officer.
• Allen Singer, B.S. (engineering), University of Colorado; Manager of corporate real estate holdings. (ret.)

—ɷ—

Today, and I hope for years to come, their friendship brightens my life and quickens my soul. To all of you: *Todah rabbah* (many, many thanks).

PHOTOS OF THINGS

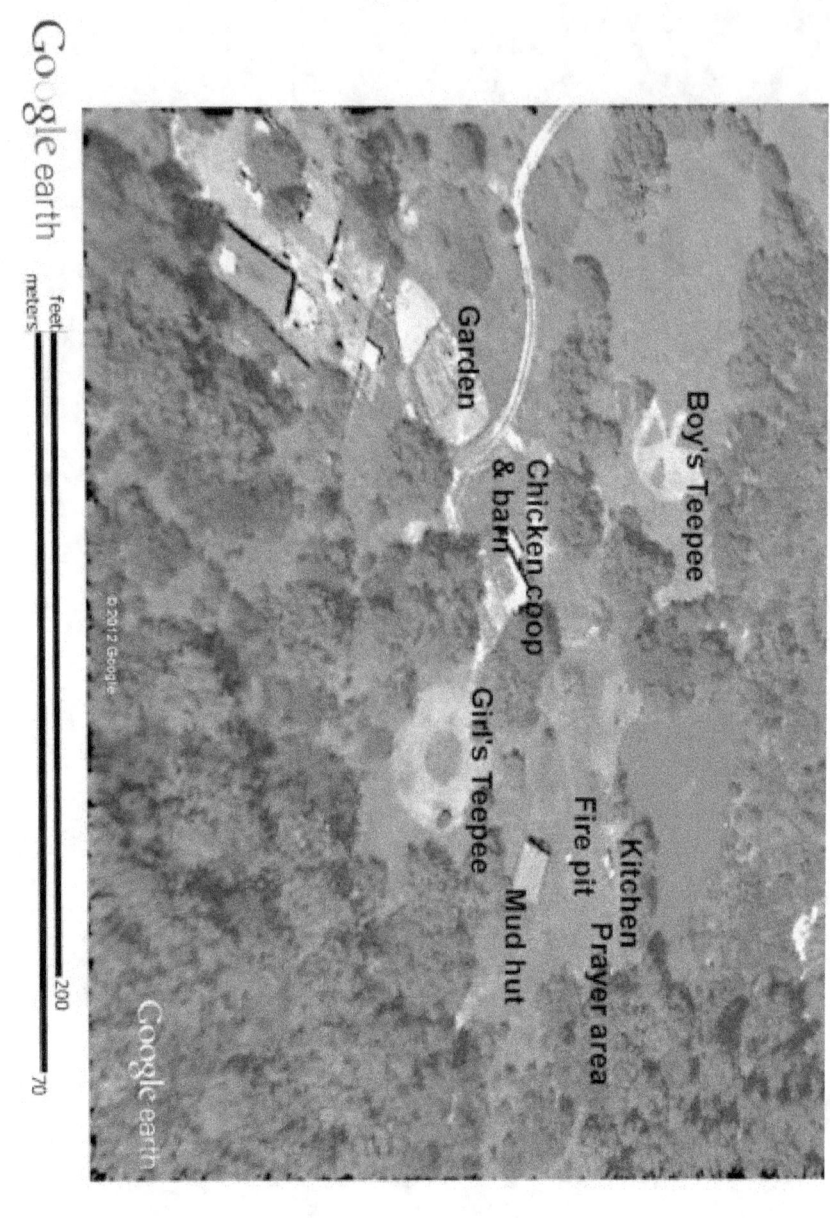

Aerial view of Kibbutz Yarok

Camp Newman's portal

Entrance to Kibbutz

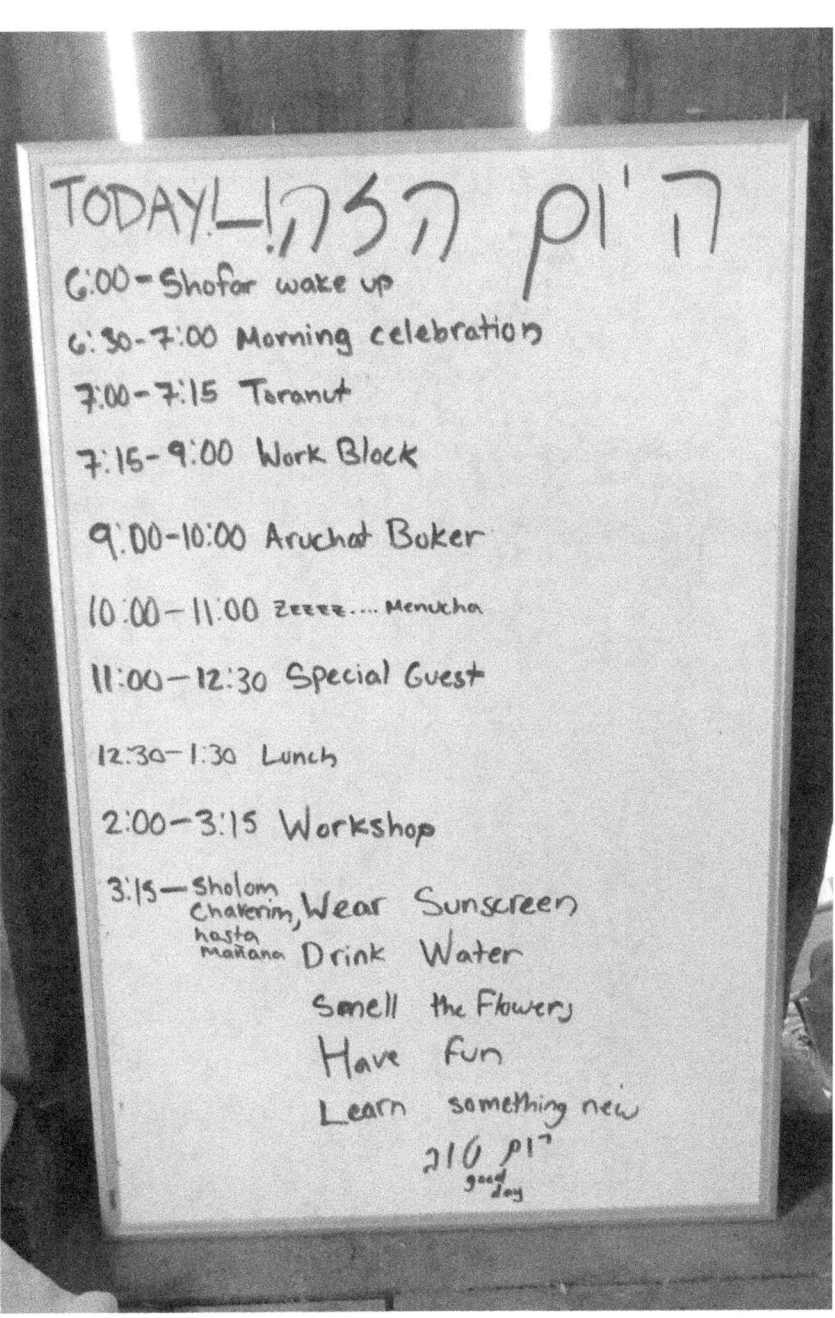

TODAY! היום הזה!

6:00 – Shofar wake up

6:30 – 7:00 Morning celebration

7:00 – 7:15 Toranut

7:15 – 9:00 Work Block

9:00 – 10:00 Aruchat Boker

10:00 – 11:00 Zzzzz.... Menucha

11:00 – 12:30 Special Guest

12:30 – 1:30 Lunch

2:00 – 3:15 Workshop

3:15 – Sholom
Chaverim, Wear Sunscreen
hasta
mañana Drink Water
Smell the Flowers
Have Fun
Learn something new
יום טוב
good
day

Day's schedule

The barn

Goats grazing

PHOTOS OF PEOPLE

EJY Board members
Front row L to R: Martin Abrams, Cheryl Lebow, Rabbi Sholom Groesberg, Lisa Katzki
Back row L to R: Allen Singer, Michael Cohen, Lillian Roselin

Ruben Arquilevich, Camp Director

Rabbi Gwasdoff and the mud hut Mezuzah

Avodahnik tends the corn crop.

Avodahniks canoeing

Prayer bench during construction

Chapter Three

THE CAMP NEWMAN STORY

A children's summer sleep-away camp is a residential facility that offers its participants a sustained experience in group outdoor living. Utilizing trained leadership, camps seek to provide creative, recreational, and educational opportunities for its campers—all within a limited time span of as little as one week, and as much as three months. Camping enables city-bred youngsters to witness the wondrous variety of the natural world: its multifaceted plant and animal life, and how humans interact with it. Involvement in outdoor living is also conducive to physical activity: a healthy antidote to the ubiquity of sedentary urban lifestyles. Camping also makes available opportunities for confronting challenges in a safe, nurturing environment; thereby building self-confidence in one's abilities. And lastly, camping is an excellent modality for attaining educational objectives.

Organized Jewish camping first appeared in the U.S. at the dawn of the 20th century. These camps belonged to two widely disparate categories. One type, the summer 'fresh air' camp, was founded as a result of the massive flood of penniless Jews that came pouring into this country from Eastern Europe during the decades 1880–1920. In that short span the number of Jews in this country increased to 4,500,000—an eighteen-fold increase. Poverty forced these immigrants to dwell in unimaginably overcrowded, squalid living quarters, which became breeding grounds for communicable diseases. The cheap-rent neighborhoods they inhabited quickly deteriorated into slums, creating all sorts of social ills. The seriousness of the situation led social welfare agencies and community groups to seek ameliorative solutions. One such measure was the establishment of free summer camps for slum-dwelling children. Fresh air camps were established by organizations in New York (1902), Detroit (1904), Cleveland (1907), and Pittsburgh (1908). By the end of the decade a dozen such camps had been founded.

The second type of Jewish camp, the 'for profit' camp, catered to affluent families who could afford to send their children to privately owned summer camps. These families wanted their scions to enjoy the amenities typical of upper-class camps from which, as a specific ethnic group, they were excluded. They wanted a camp that emulated those catering to White Anglo-Saxon Protestants (WASPS), but in which Jewish youngsters would feel welcome and comfortable. The earliest such business venture was Camp Cobbossee in Winthrop, ME (1902). Entrepreneurs were quick to recognize an opportunity, and numerous camps sprang up throughout Maine and upstate New York during that decade. Nothing could be found in these camps that remotely suggested Jewishness—other than the singularity of the clientele.

It wasn't until the 1920s that for-profit private camps—which incorporated elements of Jewish content—arose. Camp Cejwin in Port Jervis, NY (1919) was prominent among the vanguard. Established by a community center in Manhattan's Upper East Side, it served the children of middle-upper class Jewish families who wanted their offspring to become acquainted with Judaism's beliefs, practices, and values. It originated as an adjunct to a traditional type of talmud torah named the Central Jewish Institute (CJI)—from which the acronym Cejwin was created. The camp departed from CJI in one highly significant respect: All activities were conducted in English, and all were enriched with Jewish content. In time, the camp accommodated in the neighborhood of one thousand children each summer. It became the prototype of a non-Hebrew Jewish cultural camp.

Chronologically close behind came Camp Modin in Belgrade, ME (1922). It was founded by Jewish educators to serve the needs of well-to-do families seeking a 'camp with a Jewish idea'. The camp was designed to be non-denominational and pluralistic, and was built to serve as a place for campers to explore their cultural heritage and to affirm their Jewish identity. Programmatically, Modin offered Shabbat services, celebrated Bar/Bat Mitzvahs, and incorporated Israeli song and dance into its recreational activities. The camp kept kosher and the traditional blessings associated with dining were recited at mealtimes. With some 90 years of history behind it, Camp Modin is operational to this day.

The next phase in the evolution of Jewish camping followed in the wake of the massive wave of Jewish immigrants arriving from Eastern Europe. People with like-minded interests had banded together and coalesced into movements. Once solidified, leaders began thinking about socializing their members' American-born children into the respective movements. Educational summer camps thereupon sprouted. They were sponsored by a miscellany of groups: labor unions, fraternal orders, political parties, Yiddishists, Zionists. However, this type of children's camp faded away as the immigrant population became increasingly acculturated. Its successor was a new entrant: summer sleep-away camps sponsored by America's two major Jewish denominations.

In the 1940s, the Reform and Conservative movements realized that organized summer camping could counteract the deficiencies plaguing their conventional 'after public school' educational programs. Moreover, a camping experience could develop leadership skills in the youngsters, and also strengthen ideological ties to the respective religious movements.

In 1943 Rabbi Maurice Eisendrath was named to a leadership post within the Union of American Hebrew Congregations (UAHC)—the Reform movement's central administrative body. Energetic and articulate, he undertook to revitalize a movement that was patently moribund.

Among the resuscitative programs Eisendrath wished to introduce was one signaling that he had a prescient eye for the future. In 1947 he instructed the UAHC to explore the advisability of establishing summer sleep-away camps for children. Early that spring the UAHC organized an exploratory series of conclaves held in various rented camp sites for members of NFTY. The National Federation of Temple Youth was a program for encouraging college students to engage in synagogue life. The successes registered at these conclaves convinced NFTY's leadership that a permanent camp of its own was a highly desirable next step. Accordingly, a request was addressed to the UAHC urging the establishment of a committee charged with finding a suitable permanent camp site. The request was granted and the National Camp Institute Committee was formed. It decided that the search should be conducted on a regional basis, and that a nationwide network of camps ought to be the eventual goal.

Founding a camp was obviously a costly proposition. Hence Rabbi Eisendrath, at this time UAHC's president, made clear that if the movement were to establish such a network, then the regional entity involved would be obliged to supply evidence of solid local financial support for the enterprise. Given this constraint, two regions—Chicago and Northern California—decided to go ahead. In 1952, the former group succeeded in establishing a camp in Oconomowoc, WI. The venture flourished and remains a thriving institution—known as Camp Olin-Sang-Ruby Union Institute (OSRUI)—to this day.

In Northern California, thanks to the diligent and untiring efforts of a pair of Lithuanian-born rabbis, a camp was likewise founded. Raphael Levine was born in Vilna in 1901. He and his family emigrated to America eight years later, eventually settling in Duluth, MN. In quest of a career, he took a law degree and entered private practice. But having been brought up in a traditionally observant family, his vocational inclinations inexorably drew him toward the rabbinate. Eventually yielding to the impulse, he enrolled at the Reform movement's seminary—Hebrew Union College (HUC)—and received ordination in

1932. Ten years later, he accepted the pulpit at prestigious Temple de Hirsch in Seattle, WA.

Rabbi Iser Freund was born in 1895 into an Orthodox family. He received a traditional talmud torah instruction during his boyhood, and when his family emigrated to this country in 1906, he continued in that vein. As an adult, acculturated into the American way of life and thinking about a livelihood, he chose the rabbinate. He elected to attend HUC and was ordained in 1916. Ascending the congregational hierarchy of postings, in 1939 he accepted the pulpit at Congregation Emanu-el in San Jose, CA.

Once settled into Temple de Hirsch, Levine formed the Pacific Association of Reform Rabbis, a community that served to bring together his widely scattered rabbinical colleagues on the West Coast. At one of the Association's meetings he broached the idea of a summer camp for Jewish youngsters. He'd had some experience with a cross-cultural version of such a camp back in Seattle, and had been impressed with what summer camp could accomplish in the way of socialization. However, the response from his colleagues was tepid—except for Rabbi Freund who supported the suggestion enthusiastically. Accordingly, the two of them teamed up and in 1947 they rented a camp facility in the vicinity of Northern California's Lake Tahoe. Rounding up a small group of campers, the two rabbis conducted a trial run.

This initial foray was favorably received in all quarters—campers, parents, rabbis, and Jewish community leaders. The two rabbis, now functioning as camp directors, continued the program over the ensuing four summers, reconvening in rented venues within the Lake Tahoe area. Sustained encouragement from the wider Jewish community emboldened the leaders into envisioning a permanent home for the venture, and in 1953 their aspiration was actualized.

Using funds contributed by members of the San Francisco Jewish community, a 185-acre forested site in California's Santa Cruz Mountains, formerly the estate of the famous novelist Kathleen Thompson Norris, was purchased by the UAHC. The newly founded enterprise was named

Camp Saratoga because of its proximity to the town of that name. The early campers came for two- or three-week sessions during which they became acquainted with outdoor craftsmanship, shared Jewish experiences, and learned about Judaism's religious holidays and practices. A distinctive feature of the camp was the active on-site involvement of local Reform rabbis who voluntarily served as mentors and as spiritual leaders.

Increasing enrollment at the nascent Camp Saratoga attracted the attention of local philanthropist Benjamin H. Swig. Out of gratitude for a series of generous gifts, Camp Saratoga was renamed Camp Swig in the early 1950s. The infusion of cash made it possible for the camp to improve and expand its facilities substantially, with the result that enrollment grew steadily and Camp Swig continued to thrive. With each passing year, however, the camp approached closer to limitations on its further physical expansion; and with each passing year the camp's facilities aged just a bit more. In view of the fact that demand for camperships continued strong, Rabbi Allan Smith (director of the UAHC Youth Division) thought about establishing a second camp in the Northern California area. Discussions with colleagues prompted him to suggest same to the respective boards of directors of the Youth Division and of Camp Swig. They responded favorably, and decided to initiate a search by forming reconnaissance teams, which thereupon fanned out throughout the designated area in quest of a suitable site.

Meanwhile, after four laudable decades of socializing campers into Jewish ways of living, Camp Swig was jolted by a pair of hammer blows. One, the camp was informed that a portion of its property lay athwart a seismic fault line, and that buildings on this tract of land would have to be retrofitted. Two, the camp received notice that its aging infrastructure would need to be overhauled in order to comply with current building codes. In each case, corrective action was sure to be an expensive proposition. Seismic retrofitting would not come cheap, because the wood frame structures affected would require skilled workmen experienced in following code-mandated practices. And rehabilitation of the camp's infrastructure—sewage system, electrical grid, roadways—would require a sizable financial outlay in terms of labor and material. In short, Camp Swig was facing expenditures of serious dimension; or rather, the UAHC was facing them.

Although the Youth Division supervised operations, the nationwide network of camp facilities, Camp Swig included, was the property of the UAHC. In view of the manifold problems facing Camp Swig—limited camper capacity, an expensive seismic retrofit, a costly rehab of the camp's physical plant—the Youth Division, with UAHC's concurrence, prudently elected to finesse the issue. Buildings seated on the seismic fault line were closed down, and rehabilitation was put on hold. Moreover, the further reduction in camper capacity, coupled with continuing strong demand for camperships, lent new urgency to the need for a second camp.

A search had been started a while back, without turning up anything of interest. Now, with the pressure on, the search was intensified and expanded. Finally, exhaustive exploration disclosed that a satisfactory 475-acre tract in the nearby Santa Rosa Mountains was up for sale. The site had been a facility operated by the U.S. Merchant Marine during wartime for the purpose of training cooks. Professional inspection and analysis resulted in an estimated cost of 8.5 million dollars for purchase of the property and for conversion of the existing (unused) facility into a fully functional children's camp.

Inasmuch as raising the sum of 8.5 million—not a trivial amount—was the responsibility of Swig's board, one of its directors stepped forward and took an active role in the capital fund drive. Raquel Newman had been a member of Camp Swig's board of directors for some twenty years, and she fully supported the project with her time, effort, savvy—and money. Raquel herself contributed a lead donation of 1.5 million dollars. The campaign was successfully completed in 1997; whereupon, in the presence of Rabbi Eric Yoffie (UAHC's president), and Rabbi Alexander Schindler (its past president for 23 years), the new facility was formally opened. It was named Camp Newman in honor of Raquel's significant contribution to the magical process whereby a hoped-for objective was actualized into a tangible reality.

There were now two functioning sister camps located about one hundred miles apart. Newman had not yet appointed a camp executive director; while Swig already had one in place: Ruben Arquilevich was in his third year in the position. Although this was his first experience at such a senior level of responsibility—he had previously been an assistant executive director at a Jewish Community Center (JCC) camp in Los Angeles—he had been performing commendably at Swig. Consequently, for the sake of operational efficiency, and with an eye on the fiscal bottom line, both camps were placed under his administrative leadership. He accepted the daunting assignment because he was confident he could assemble a capable leadership team for each of the facilities. He himself would split his time between the two. Thus was born the hyphenated Camp Swig-Newman.

In order to avoid needless duplication, the two camps offered programs directed at different age groups. Camp Swig, given its smaller capacity—reduced still further by closing off buildings seated on the seismic fault—focused on programming for teenagers. Camp Newman, given its potential for substantial expansion, offered programs for third through seventh graders. From time to time, as appropriate, selected events were conducted jointly.

Meanwhile, amidst the celebratory mood created by the advent of Camp Newman, the dreaded day of reckoning for Camp Swig arrived. Civic authorities had ordered it to bring its facility into compliance with extant health and environmental standards—or close down. The UAHC, owner of the property, was faced with an unenviable situation. Making the necessary renovations (buildings, sewers, electrical grid, roads) in order to keep Swig operational would impose a staggering financial burden. Exacerbating the problem was the fact that Camp Newman still had a sizable mortgage to pay off. But Newman was a completely refurbished facility and had twice the capacity of aged Camp Swig. Sober analysis indicated that the prudent course of action was to put the Swig property up for sale.

A storm of protests immediately erupted. Loyal alumni vigorously and vociferously objected to any sale of their beloved Camp Swig. Whereupon the UAHC showed them facts and figures, and tactfully suggested that the irate loyalists step up to the plate and raise some sort of rescue fund. This they energetically set about doing; at which point it was discovered that pledges were one thing, but cash on the barrelhead was another. Apparently, this was a case of—as Texans would say—'big hat, no cattle'. So the UAHC resumed its efforts to sell the property.

In 1998, one year after Camp Newman came into being, Rembrandt Venture Partners, a Silicon Valley consortium of venture capital investors, made an unsolicited bid of $3.9 million for the Camp Swig property. They purportedly had in mind a retreat center and a winery. But while negotiations were going on, they withdrew the bid without explanation. So it was back to the status ante. Then, an anonymous $2 million gift materialized and the skies brightened. The entire sum, according to the director of UAHC's Northern California region, would be allocated toward helping get Swig up to speed as a summer camp. However, he added, more substantial improvements might ultimately require more money. The hope was that additional donations would follow this lead gift, but nothing substantial was forthcoming.

Meanwhile, aware of the financial situation, various Bay Area groups (e.g., the Jewish Federation of Greater San Jose; and HaMakom, a collectivity of local rabbis and camp alumni) launched attempts to raise the $4 million needed to buy the camp. But the response to these campaigns was anemic and the sputtering initiatives soon evaporated. Then in 2003, the effort to sell the property took on added urgency due to a fire at Swig the previous year. Estimates regarding restoration made clear that the repairs would require sums stretching into the millions. Accordingly, the camp was closed down, but the property was still there. So it once again went on the market in 2007, and efforts to affect a sale resumed. The Union for Reform Judaism (URJ)—in 2003 the movement had officially changed its name from UAHC—soon received a bid of $5 million from a Jewish group. However, during negotiations an offer of $6 million was tendered by a Methodist Church group which planned to turn the property into a Christian retreat center. Citing 'financial due diligence', the URJ accepted the higher bid. Anger and dismay spread among community leaders over the projected sale. They were appalled by the idea that the Reform movement would prefer to sell the property to a non-Jewish group, even though a Jewish group had offered to buy it for $5 million.

But then a stunning turnabout occurred. The real estate market at the time was in the midst of a serious downturn, and the Methodist Church group had counted on selling one of its properties in order to raise the necessary Swig purchase price. When that sale fell through, however, the Swig deal had to be canceled; thereby reviving the possibility that the camp might remain in Jewish hands. So, back the property went on the market. In 2010, a Silicon Valley entrepreneur tendered a bid of $4.9 million for the property. Her intention was to establish a 500-student interfaith boarding school. The bid was accepted, the deal consummated, and thus Camp Swig was no more.

Loyal Swig alumni were far from pleased. During the fifty summers of Swig's existence, campers had stored memories of many happy experiences in their emotional baggage. Thus, their loyalty to Swig was strong indeed. And, as reality makes clear, financial support by alumni is largely contingent on emotional factors. Consequently, Newman's administrators astutely decided that given the psychological importance of names—the universal seat of identity—a gradual ten-year transition process would be implemented. Thus, proceeding as circumspectly as possible, Camp Swig became Swig-Newman, became Newman-Swig, became Camp Newman. The strategy proved to be inordinately effective as evidenced by the fact that involvement in Newman's affairs by alumni from every period in the half-century of Swig/Newman's existence continued to be broad-based and enthusiastic. Swig's praiseworthy history remains as a legacy for Newman. All the old camp rituals remain in place, refurbished as necessary. All the artistic artifacts that once adorned various Swig sites have been transferred to Newman for safe-keeping until such time as suitable repositories become available. And the *ru'ach* (spiritedness) that once pervaded Swig continues unabated in Newman. It manifests itself in every aspect of Newman's efflorescence, and will exert its salutary influence far into the future.

All the while, under whatever formal name, the camp continued to grow apace. In response to escalating demand for camperships, capacity was increased from 500 to 700 beds. Exciting new activities and programs were continually being developed. For example, younger campers could participate in activities such as Martial Arts, or Digital Video, or Zip-line travel. Teenagers could elect to participate in a new program that focused on exploring ecological issues in the wild. Another new program employed interactive teenage focus groups for the purpose of examining issues related to social justice.

Year after year, Camp Newman continued to move the enterprise forward. For example, in 2011 the administration reported that approximately 1,500 campers were accommodated; supervised by roughly 300 counselors and staffers; assisted by something on the order of 80 rabbis, physicians, and artists who voluntarily serve two-week stints at Newman. In addition, at events it sponsored during the nine months when camp was not in session, Newman hosted approximately 5,000 adults and children at various retreats.

A further propitious development was the decision by Newman's board of directors—approved by the Reform movement's Youth Division—to completely renovate a facility (the school for cooks) first built in the 1940s. A three-year plan of performance was developed, and a $30 million capital fund drive launched.

Camp Newman has shown itself to be an exemplar within the URJ's national constellation of children's camps. Under the inspiring leadership of an executive director, ably assisted by an adroit and nimble staff, generously supported by philanthropic agencies and alumni, and staunchly buttressed by an activist board—all concerned can justifiably be proud of what Newman has achieved in fulfilling its mission:

> To enrich and transform lives by strengthening Jewish identity, teaching Jewish knowledge, instilling Jewish values and cultivating lifelong friendships within a vibrant and fun community of living Judaism.

To the many, many individuals who have contributed in some way to the success story that is Camp Newman: *Shalom uv'rachah!* May you be granted peace and blessing!

Chapter Four

THE GENESIS OF
KIBBUTZ YAROK

Ruben Arquilevich's earliest recollection of encountering the word 'kibbutz' he traces back to a time when he was eight years of age (or thereabouts). His parents, immigrants fleeing from Eastern Europe, had thankfully found a haven in Argentina and had settled in Cordoba. Ruben was born in 1962, and one year later, in hope of a more complaisant life, the family relocated to Los Angeles.

Siblings of Ruben's parents, similarly in quest of a haven, had opted for Israel. Thus, Ruben had lots of aunts, uncles, and cousins in that country, and his family often visited in order to reconnect with relatives. So Ruben got to spend a bit of time at the various places where the relatives lived: at the seashore north of Tel Aviv, at a residential neighborhood in Ashkelon, and at assorted cooperative agricultural communities known as *kibbutzim*. During his family's customary visits to Israel, the stopovers at kibbutzim made a lasting impression upon young Ruben. He was captivated by their way of life. Unlike his hometown of Los Angeles, it was the great outdoors surrounded by unlimited greenery. A huge bunch of kids, knowing one another, were running about freely. There was no crowdedness or decay, only growth and freshness. This was a *community*, where everyone ate together and worked together. As invariably happens with significant life experiences, this one burrowed its way into his consciousness.

Meanwhile, Ruben was growing up, doing well in his high school studies, and acquiring some Jewish learning in a supplementary afternoon 'Hebrew school'. As the son of immigrant parents, he understood the importance of finding some sort of remunerative occupation. And in his mind this translated into obtaining a college education, the cost of which his family could ill afford. In a conversation with his high school advisor regarding the possibility of obtaining a scholarship, it was suggested that he try Colorado College: a small, highly selective, private college with Christian roots. This was an era, the advisor mentioned, when 'diversity' was a popular catchword in elite liberal arts college circles. And Ruben certainly filled the bill: personable, foreign born, an athlete, excellent high school credentials, and *Jewish*. The college accepted him, and offered a generous 75% scholarship.

A three-quarter free ride was undoubtedly welcome. But Ruben preferred not to burden his family with the annual obligation of scraping together the remaining 25%. Accordingly, he worked for three summers as a counselor at a Christian Scientist camp (one-third of whose kids were Jewish!) The camp director, impressed by the skill and enthusiasm with which Ruben fulfilled his duties, suggested he consider making some aspect of camp work his vocation. Although he was a pre-med major, upon graduation he followed the camp director's advice and voluntarily worked for a year at the camp clearing out existing hiking trails and laying out new ones. He found the experience highly fulfilling—Ruben had found his life's work.

Returning to L.A., Ruben set about fashioning a career in camp management. Already possessing a baccalaureate degree from Colorado College, he decided to augment that with an MBA degree. In response to his innate ethnic grounding, he matriculated at the University of Judaism—now known as the American Jewish University. In this way he could pursue the MBA degree while concurrently minoring in Jewish

Studies. Now properly credentialed, he found a position as assistant administrative director at Camp Shalom, a summer sleep-away camp in Malibu, CA, sponsored by the Los Angeles JCC. While there, Ruben received a thorough grounding in the responsibilities associated with managing a summer camp. One minor facet of camp life particularly impressed him: Older campers could voluntarily choose to work at cleaning up and beautifying the camp grounds. He was impressed by the willingness of teenagers to engage in community service, and to do so with enthusiasm. This display of selflessness embedded itself in some crevice of his brain.

In 1994, Ruben received a phone call from Rabbi Allan Smith, director of UAHC's Youth Division. Apparently, word about talented people gets around quickly. Rabbi Smith advised Ruben that due to a resignation, the position of executive director at Camp Swig was now open. Invited to apply, Ruben did so, and was chosen from among the seven candidates. Whereupon he and his family relocated to the Bay Area and Ruben assumed his new post at Camp Swig.

While getting accustomed to things at his new posting, he discovered that there actually existed on its grounds something resembling a kibbutz! It was off by itself, there were tents for overnight sleeping, campers spoke Hebrew, and they tended gardens. The idea of a proto-typical kibbutz, by and for American youngsters, was always reposing fitfully within his subconscious. At this point Ruben resolved to develop the existing nucleus of a kibbutz into a full-fledged model of an Israeli kibbutz. While ideas regarding ways and means were germinating in his mind, Camp Newman was founded in 1997. Ruben was appointed director of both camps and his oversized plate was filled to overflow-ing. Staffs at the two camps had to be appointed, programs developed, administrative bodies supervised, and everything integrated. Moreover, all the convolutions associated with the Swig property were demanding Ruben's attention. Reluctantly, he was obliged to put on hold his dream of an on-site kibbutz. It wasn't till five years later, in 2001, that Ruben's dream was rekindled. His workload had eased to the point where, quotidian obligations permitting, Ruben could take walking tours in order to reconnoiter the property adjacent to Camp Newman.

On one such jaunt he inspected a building that latterly had been the residence of one of Newman's year-round caretakers. Further inquiry revealed that the property Newman now possessed had long ago been a working ranch and this building had been the ranch house. Nearby was a seedy, but sturdily constructed barn—probably likewise a relic of the old Wilson Ranch. The ranch house had been rehabilitated into the caretaker's residence, but the barn had suffered from neglect and needed to be repaired. Continuing his inspection, Ruben discovered something he had not noticed before. Hidden by a stand of trees was a small pond completely glutted with aquatic growth. House, pond, barn—the nucleus of a kibbutz was right there. The terrain was attractive in terms of variety: hills, meadows, forests, meandering stream. Moreover, there was in place a dirt roadway that connected the caretakers' residence with Camp Newman. His vision—a self-sustaining, eco-friendly, and self-governing community in which campers could sojourn for a short stay—now acquired the lineaments of an actualized reality.

He soon commenced discussing the idea with associates, evaluating their ideas in the context of his own. Encouraged by their support, in 2005 a proposal was submitted to Newman's board of directors and to Paul Reichenbach, the director of URJ's Youth Division. The document outlined the objectives of the experimental project and a program for implementing same. All the principals involved approved of the plan; with one important proviso attached. Newman, shouldering a heavy mortgage, could not afford to divert any of its financial reserves to fully supporting the kibbutz; it would have to find a substantial portion of its support from independent sources.

As detailed in Chapter Two, negotiations between the Endowment for Jewish Youth and Camp Newman eventuated in a Memorandum of Understanding. Newman would annually submit a report and a projected budget on behalf of the kibbutz; the kibbutz, in turn, would receive a $20,000 grant from EJY. The necessary funding having been assured, Ruben appeared once more before Newman's board and obtained approval for a mutually satisfactory modus operandi. Newman agreed to set aside 20 acres of its property—the location that had caught Ruben's eye—to serve as the kibbutz site. Additionally, Newman agreed to lend the kibbutz equipment and a work crew as needed, and to cover the cost of a technical consultant, selected by the kibbutz staff, to assist in building the project. The ideal choice would be an English-speaking member of an Israeli Kibbutz affiliated with the Reform movement, of which there were two: Kibbutz Yahel and Kibbutz Lotan.

—〜〜—

In the 1960s, an affiliate of Reform Judaism was established in the holy land, and named itself the Israel Movement for Progressive Judaism (IMPJ). That the Reform movement had any sort of presence in the Jewish state was an achievement because at every step it faced intransigent opposition from Orthodoxy. Eighty per cent of Israeli Jews identify themselves as secular; only twenty per cent identify as religious. Yet as a result of some ill-advised politicking when the state was born, Orthodoxy gained full control over all matters of a religious nature. Moreover, their rulings were binding on all Israeli Jews; including the 80 per cent who identified themselves as secular. It's interesting to note that in naming the new group the Israeli leadership preferred 'Progressive' over 'Reform'. This was because the state's entrenched Orthodoxy so zealously vilified and harassed American Reform (as it still does), that in the Israeli mind the term 'Reform' connoted something excessively demeaning. Nonetheless, the IMPJ took root, grew despite ceaseless obstructionism, and is today widely recognized as a progressive alternative to proscription-obsessed Orthodoxy.

At its inception, the nascent IMPJ was wrestling with the problem of how to attract to its ranks Israeli young men and women. The organization's leadership felt that establishing a kibbutz would be an effective strategy. But such a venture would require some heavy-duty support, and so the UAHC was contacted. In 1970, representatives from IMPJ and UAHC met at the seminar center of a teachers college established by Israel's kibbutz movement. The two principals agreed that the kibbutz ought to be a project involving both American and Israeli young men and women who would jointly found and build the kibbutz.

Negotiations were initiated with the Jewish Agency (JA), the governmental organization responsible for the absorption of new immigrants. The Agency welcomed the proposed project and the three principals involved—UAHC, IMPJ, and JA—first tackled the issue of situating the new kibbutz. The Agency, in the interest of security and economic development, preferred a location in one of the country's outlying regions: the West Bank in the east, the Galilee in the north, the Negev in the south. The Reform representatives vetoed the West Bank because of ideological objections to the occupation. As for the Galilee, it already had its fair share of established kibbutzim. Therefore, the three principals agreed on a site located at the eastern-most edge of the arid Negev, close to the border with Jordan. There was something exhilarating about the choice: not only would the kibbutz be settling the land, it would also contribute to 'making the desert bloom'. In 1976, a group of fifty-five Jewish young men and women, recruited chiefly from UAHC's youth groups in America and from IMPJ's Leo Baeck School in Haifa, launched Kibbutz Yahel. It was an ecologically based enterprise dedicated to the principles of communal living and to the ideology of Progressive Judaism.

The obstacles these pioneers faced were daunting. This cadre of young American and *sabra* (Israeli-born) Jews had settled in a broiling, windswept corner of the southeast Negev Desert. The soil was hardscrabble and water was scarce. Any attempt at human habitation, and establishment of an agriculturally based collective, was a defiant challenge to both reason and to nature. Furthermore, Yahel's site was distant from both of the closest outposts of civilization: 60 miles from the city of Eilat to the south; 90 miles from the Dead Sea—a popular destination for visitors—to the north. Their present social environment was a far cry from what they had known in Haifa and the United States.

The success they achieved in creating a permanent, viable community was a highly impressive achievement. Furthermore, it served as an inspiration. The triumvirate that engineered the first success decided to replicate it. In 1983, using the same planning model as before, Yahel II was launched by a contingent of twenty American and twenty Israeli youths on a site eight miles south of Yahel I. Due to their shared parentage and geographical proximity, a sort of 'sibling rivalry' developed between the two kibbutzim. First off, the younger sibling wanted an identity of its own, and so the name was changed from Kibbutz Yahel II to Kibbutz Lotan. Secondly, Lotan was more in tune with socialistic ideals than its older sibling, and more observant in terms of Shabbat and *kashrut*. Despite differences, however, the two kibbutzim cooperated willingly and often. As of this writing, both Yahel and Lotan are alive and well. All things considered, the Reform movement can take pride in its accomplishment.

—w—

Meanwhile, Ruben's vision of a kibbutz as an adjunct to Camp Newman was taking shape. The financial support was there and in hand. The requested 20-acre site had been allocated. Newman's board had agreed to cover the cost of a technical consultant. Whereupon Ruben decided to launch the kibbutz project the following summer, the summer of 2009. The facility was named Kibbutz Yarok, and operational management of the facility was designated OKY (Operation Kibbutz Yarok). Ari Vared, a longtime associate thoroughly familiar with the ins and outs of camp life, was named Yarok's executive director.

Next on the agenda was finding a technical consultant. Ruben wanted someone from either of Reform's kibbutzim, Yahel or Lotan, who was also knowledgeable in matters related to building a kibbutz from the ground up. Then he remembered that while attending a conference in Palm Springs for regional Reform rabbis—some of whom often served as 'guest faculty' at Newman—one of the rented booths had been occupied by a delegation from Kibbutz Lotan. He chatted with them, picked up some of the literature on display, and when leaving he accepted their invitation to visit. While on many of his family's frequent sojourns in Israel, he had often planned to drop by Lotan—only to be deterred by one circumstance or another. At any rate, he decided to hire someone from that kibbutz.

In past years Ruben had invariably hired Israeli kibbutzniks to serve as counselors and staffers for Camp Newman's summer sessions. Their presence immeasurably enhanced the quality of camp life, both Jewishly and in terms of the role models the Israelis represented. Many Jewish camps in the U.S., for similar reasons, also hired Israelis for the summer. Accordingly, an agency representing the kibbutz movement annually compiled a list of applicants, included a brief bio for each, and distributed the list to interested American camps; one of which was Camp Newman.

For the summer of 2009 Ruben noted that the list included some-one from Kibbutz Lotan. Perusing his bio and inquiring around, Ruben learned that Ido Ma'or was considered personable, had a good command of English, was a conscientious worker, and knew about construction. He was patently the technical consultant Yarok was looking for. The necessary permissions were obtained, arrangements between Newman and Lotan were finalized, and Ido joined Yarok for its inaugural summer.

Once settled in, the first task facing Ari Vared and Ido Ma'or was the development of a slate of programs for that summer. The list they promulgated included building a Lotan-style mud hut, planting an organic vegetable garden, constructing an outdoor cook-place, and mak-ing a mud bench for the proposed outdoor prayer site. This was indeed an ambitious program, and bringing it to completion would have been unrealizable were it not for the active participation of the volunteer work crew: the avodahniks.

At its conclusion, OKY's inaugural summer was evaluated. The results were commendable, considering that this was a start-up opera-tion, and that the work crew consisted largely of untried camp teenagers.

The immediate grounds had been cleared of long-accumulated brush and debris strewn about everywhere. The pond had been cleared of aquatic growth (as evidenced by the sight of campers leisurely paddling about in a pair of canoes). The smaller projects—a cook space, a dining table, a mud bench—had all been completed according to plan. The walls of a six by eight foot mud hut had been built, but the roof had yet to be constructed. The organic vegetable garden was a decided success. Thanks to a substantial investment of labor in battling the intractable hardscrabble soil, the avodahniks had the satisfaction of seeing their garden produce a bountiful crop of zucchini, tomatoes, cucumbers, lettuce, and onions. Furthermore, much of their produce turned up at meal time as ingredients in culinary *chef-d'oeuvres* prepared by Newman's kitchen staff.

Aside from the tangible accomplishments, there was much else to feel good about. Self-esteem all around was heightened by the realization that 'we can get things done'. In addition, both staffers and campers had learned about such things as topography, infrastructure, renewable resources, construction techniques, and organic gardening. In sum, the evidence demonstrated that neonatal Kibbutz Yarok had done quite well merely by making it through its first summer.

When the crew of OKY staffers reassembled in advance of 2010's summer session, what they saw was far from exhilarating. The mud hut was still there, but in poor condition. Sections of the foundation had given way and the hut was standing aslant. Also, the walls were not quite straight, and here and there pieces had fallen away. The cook space had weathered seriously and would require rebuilding. And the garden plots, so lovingly tended the previous summer, were choked with weeds, while the soil had reverted to its hardscrabble condition.

These disappointments should have been expected. The first year of newborn Kibbutz Yarok's existence amounted to little more than a shakedown cruise. True, it had the help of staffers thoroughly experienced in running Camp Newman. But in Yarok, staffers were entering upon unfamiliar terrain. Their prior Newman experience was useful to an appreciable degree, but now there was a significant difference in the operational circumstances: Newman was long-established and staff-driven; whereas Yarok was a start-up and camper-driven. Cognizant of this relevant detail, Ruben was not disheartened. Rallying the somewhat dispirited crew—now beneficiaries of hard-earned hindsight—they figured out what went wrong and how to rectify things. The mud hut's foundation was buttressed at points where sagging had occurred; walls were protected against spalling by applying an oil-based coating; and a peaked wood roof, standing free of the hut itself, was constructed. The cook space was rebuilt, but this time using sturdier support posts solidly implanted in the ground. The garden plots were weeded, reconditioned, and measures taken to counteract the clayey soil's poor irrigational properties.

A number of new projects—more modest in scope than the previous year's list—were also undertaken. Mud benches were added to the prayer space, a picnic area was set out, and a few movable wood benches were built from Newman scrap lumber. Perhaps this did not seem like much for eight weeks of effort. However, all things considered, the results were quite respectable. But Ruben, ever the realist, recognized that his vision for Yarok could not be realized unless a fundamental policy change was made. OKY could not remain a three-month activity; it was essential that OKY become a viable *year-round* operation. This necessitated finding a qualified full-time program director who'd be resident on the kibbutz site 12 months a year.

The quest for a resident program director yielded results a lot sooner than expected. Back in 2008, Sophie Vener was serving as a floating camp specialist at Camp Newman responsible for assisting in activities related to environmentalism. When Ruben decided to start up the kibbutz in 2009, he got busy assembling a staff. As he was acquainted with Sophie's qualifications, she was among those selected to serve as a staffer for the project's inaugural summer. Midway through the season—entirely out of the blue—Sophie told Ruben about a dream she'd had: She would be living year-round in the unoccupied house on the camp site, developing programs for OKY. Ruben was astounded. This was precisely the person he was hoping to find for the position of resident program director! Sophie possessed all the necessary credentials. Having been a Newman staffer, she was familiar with life at camp. Ruben knew from first-hand observation that she was endowed with excellent people skills. She had sojourned in Israel more than once, and had studied at Kibbutz Lotan. And having come up through its youth movement, she was well acquainted with Reform's principles and practices. Ruben thereupon suggested that if she was sincerely interested, it might be a good idea for them to explore this further.

Subsequent discussions went well and at one point Sophie asked Ruben about the possibility of being joined by a second person in order to share the duties of year-round program directors. She and Persephone Rivka had met briefly when both were involved in a program teaching leadership skills to NFTY teenagers at URJ's Camp Kutz (Warwick, NY). More recently, they had at different times completed the eight-week permaculture course offered at Kibbutz Lotan, and both had been credentialed. Sophie suggested that the two, working jointly in planning and implementing OKY programs, could make for an efficient team. Ruben was amenable to the idea, and asked Sophie to set up an interview. Soon afterwards, the two young women met with OKY's senior staffers for a get-acquainted session. During the interview the applicants set forth their view that Kibbutz Yarok's healthy development could best be facilitated if guided by principles based on permaculture's approach to agriculture and Judaism's approach to ethicality. Ruben and his staffers, accepting the suggested operational modality, commenced negotiating administrative and contractual issues.

The arrangements that were agreed upon satisfied all parties involved. The two new staffers would live year-round, rent-free, in the ranch house (the former caretaker's quarters) located on the kibbutz site. They themselves would make it more habitable—and much needed to be done—at no cost to Yarok. They would receive a modest annual stipend to cover living expenses. They would be permitted to take limited time off during the 'off-season' in order to resume studies that had been interrupted because of their assorted peregrinations. And so Sophie Vener and Persephone Rivka came on board as Kibbutz Yarok's new program directors. Ruben was delighted with the felicitous outcome of his quest. As he expressed it: "It was *bashert* (Yiddish for 'destined')." But perhaps it was also an augury of his hopes for Kibbutz Yarok's future. Perhaps destiny was indeed on his side and his cherished dream would eventually be realized. The project had survived the first year, and had made the necessary course corrections during the second year. Things were clearly headed in the right direction. As all the principals involved saw it, the genesis of Kibbutz Yarok had factually been brought to successful completion. Ruben could take well-deserved satisfaction in his accomplishment. His dream had been transmuted into a reality. In the memorable words of Theodor Herzl: *Im tirtzu, ein zo aggadah.* "If you will it, it is no dream."

Chapter Five

THE VISION TAKES SHAPE

*T*he first summer of Kibbutz Yarok's existence could best be described as an exploratory expedition. It had its share of mistakes, wrong turns, and slip-ups. But it was a valuable, perhaps necessary, learning experience, inasmuch as things were set aright and Yarok was able to move ahead during the second summer. Now in its third year, the project was ready to move forward. Two on-site year-round residents, Sophie Vener and Persephone Rivka, were on board as program directors. They were joined in their deliberations by Joe Glass, newly appointed executive director of Kibbutz Yarok. His predecessor, Ari Vared, had been upgraded to a managerial position assisting Newman in its $30 million capital fund drive. Although Joe was resident year-round at Camp Newman, he split his time between camp and kibbutz as circumstances dictated.

In putting together a plan of performance for 2011, the calendrical year was divided into a three-month 'on-season' when the kibbutz was fully operational, and a nine-month 'off-season' when matters ancillary to Operation Kibbutz Yarok (OKY) could be attended to. Heading the agenda were programs to be undertaken during the 'on-season'. First came those projects which had previously been started, but which merely needed to be carried forward. This brought the agenda to new stuff for the summer. Considerations such as budgetary concerns, resource availability, and time constraints seriously impacted whatever decisions were made. Therefore, Sophie, Persephone, and Joe thought it prudent if they functioned as a committee of three in developing a plan of performance. What emerged from their deliberations was a consensual agreement that four major areas of activity merited focused attention: I. Expanding OKY's capacity for growing produce; II. Generating additional revenue streams; III. Making the kibbutz suitable for round-the-clock residency; and IV. Building up the 'off season' occupancy rate.

This was indeed an ambitious list of projects. However, the committee did not let the 'big picture' obscure less conspicuous, but equally worthy, objectives. They saw fit to place on the 2011 agenda a handful of smaller projects, principally: construction of box ovens that could use either the sun's rays or the burning of wood as a heat source; beautification of the Yarok facility by planting trees and creating strategically placed decorative art; and development of an outdoor dining area consisting of a field kitchen plus tables and benches shaded by an awning.

Confronted by the magnitude of the proposed summer agenda, Sophie and Persephone recognized that they themselves could not carry the burden; Joe Glass was able to lend a hand only whenever he was free from responsibilities at Newman. Thus, successful implementation of the plan of performance could not be realized unless additional experienced hands were added to the team. But this implied an expenditure that had not been anticipated, and therefore had not been budgeted. At this juncture, serendipity came to the rescue in the form of two volunteers, each possessing valuable experience as well as equable temperaments.

Sophie was enrolled at Santa Rosa Junior College, and taking classes offered at Shone Farm, an adjunct facility that is part of the college's agricultural program. Also enrolled in one of those classes was Angelo Silva. He grew up in San Diego, which also happens to be Sophie's hometown. They became friends, traded histories, and he found out about OKY. Inasmuch as he had been involved in the world of organic agriculture for the past three years, he was curious about what was happening at Kibbutz Yarok. He visited, liked what he saw, and volunteered to lend a helping hand from time to time. For Angelo the OKY experience was quite fulfilling in terms of his vocational interests, and before too long he realized that he'd like to be involved on a less transitory basis. Discussions followed and an arrangement was subsequently worked out with Joe Glass whereby, in exchange for lodging, Angelo would work on the kibbutz for twelve hours a week.

A second new helper was Jen Swanson. Sophie and Persephone had met her at a Chanukah party. Chit-chat led to an exchange of life-stories and there seemed to be some parallels in their respective pathways. For example, Jen had been a staffer at a summer sleep-away camp sponsored by the San Francisco JCC: Camp Tawonga located near Yosemite National Park. Tawonga was thus kin to Camp Newman in mission, campership, and style. Further, while a student at Washington University (St. Louis, MO), Jen helped start up an urban farm camp. This was similar to what Sophie had done while a student at Wheaton College (Norton, MA). Upshot of these congruities: Jen came aboard via a work-lodging arrangement similar to Angelo's. Now that OKY's two program directors could count on the assistance of Angelo and Jen, all of the impending summer's four planned major projects became pragmatically realizable.

I. Increasing vegetable productivity.
The objective of the first project was to increase the output of the organic vegetable gardens. Such produce represented, for Kibbutz Yarok, a highly remunerative cash crop; moreover, it was an annually recurring income generator. Increasing vegetable garden productivity could be achieved by means of two strategies. The first involved increasing the acreage allotted to vegetable gardening. Accordingly, during the off-season a perimeter fence was erected enclosing a projected area that effectively tripled the garden's existing size.

The second strategy was more complicated and therefore more difficult to implement. It focused on maximizing—under the constraints imposed by limited money, time, and labor resources—the gardens' crop yield. The chief impediment was something the kibbutz had inherited: poor soil quality. A lab analysis done at the community college Sophie was attending showed that the soil sample was doubly deficient—low in nutritive value and high in clay content. Nutritive minerals such as nitrogen, phosphorus, and potassium are essential for efficient photosynthesis. As for clay, it is impervious to water, which is crucial in supporting the photosynthetic cycle.

Three steps were taken in an attempt to mitigate these deficiencies. First, cover crops were planted which would be plowed under in the spring. The decomposing vegetation would thereby add nutrients to the soil. Second, food leftovers from Newman's kitchen were collected, sorted into usable and unusable heaps, and the former was delivered to Yarok for building compost piles. (Compost is decayed organic material, such as food, which is rich in nutrients and thus serves as fertilizer.) Third, mulch sheets were prepared and laid atop garden beds. Simple and cheap to make, a layer of cardboard is placed atop a section of soil. Then a layer of leaf detritus is added. Lastly, a layer of straw is spread on top to complete the 'sandwich'. Mulch sheets make stored nutrients slowly available to seeds sown below. They also provide a habitat for earthworms, which are excellent soil conditioners. Furthermore, sheet mulching can serve as a selective herbicide by blocking the sunlight needed to support the growth of deleterious plants.

The above-mentioned strategies were implemented in two phases: preparatory activities done during the 'off-season', followed by work performed during the summer 'on-season' related to building the kibbutz. In the fall, while the weather was still warm, garden beds were loosened up to improve permeability and cover crops were planted. Additionally, while digging was still comparatively easy, some purchased trees were implanted—trees anchor the soil, contribute to water retention, act as windbreaks, and provide shade.

Once the cold winter weather set in, gardening articles that could be made indoors—protective shade panels, starter flat-bed trays, support trellises—were fabricated. Also, a rudimentary greenhouse for growing seedlings was constructed out of a low-cost storage shed in which metal surfaces were replaced by translucent panels.

In the spring, activities were focused mainly on readying the vegetable garden beds for summer sowing. Conditioning of the soil was started. Seeds, fertilizer, tools, and general gardening paraphernalia were purchased. For selected vegetable varietals needing a head-start, seedlings were gotten going in flat-bed trays. Also, work was begun on building a compost pile.

Summer was the season during which—thanks to the avodahniks' collective efforts—nine months of gardening prep time materialized as cash crop. The soil was tilled; most often by hand plowing, but sometimes by mechanical means when Yarok could get its hands on a power tiller. Next came the seed (or seedling) implantation procedure, which varied in accordance with the vegetable being grown. Then mulch sheets were laid down. Afterwards, throughout the growing cycle, garden beds were weeded, protected from pests, and irrigated as necessary. Finally, produce was selectively harvested as it ripened.

All of Kibbutz Yarok—staffers, avodahniks, counselors, CITs— gloried in what had been accomplished that summer of 2011. They had harvested a bumper crop of organically grown vegetables, sufficient to feed the kibbutz itself and to selectively provision Newman's kitchen. Moreover, there was still enough left over so that Yarok was able to donate vegetables to the Santa Rosa food bank.

II. Expanding revenue streams.

It was generally understood by all principals involved that a robust set of revenue streams was a *sine qua non* if Kibbutz Yarok hoped to establish itself as a viable and enduring community. All agreed that progress to date had been promising. Organically grown vegetables were patently the backbone of this effort. But nothing prevented Yarok from expanding its gardening enterprise beyond vegetable crops. The notion persisted that niche markets existed for other organically garden-grown crops. One possibility was berries. Deliciously sweet blackberries grew wild and in abundance on the kibbutz site. It was therefore reasonable to suppose that conditions were similarly suitable for growing other berry species—strawberries, blueberries, raspberries. Fresh berries in season, as well as home-made jars of jam, might turn out to be eminently marketable. Another possibility was herbs. At the request of Newman's cooks, a small selection had been grown on-site, and had served quite nicely as herbal complements to their culinary creations. Cultivation of organically grown herbs could easily be expanded into a profitable sideline. And lest it be overlooked, how about getting fresh flowers to nearby markets while in full bloom?

Fruit trees were also regarded as a promising income producer. In fact, OKY's program directors had fruit trees on their agenda from the very beginning. Local experts had been consulted about particulars concerning what to grow, and when, and where. The best candidates turned out to be apple, pear, apricot, and plum. The idea was to plant five-tree groves in suitable locations throughout Yarok's 20-acre site. Angelo reconnoitered the kibbutz grounds during off-hours in search of suitable locales. Factoring in features such as irrigation, tillage, sunshine, and soil quality, he pinpointed prospective suitable spots for groves. He also suggested considering an additional varietal of fruit tree that would be very capable of producing a nice cash crop: trees producing edible nuts of marketable quality.

Aside from vegetative contributions to revenue streams, a second potentially profitable source of income—a source derived from animal husbandry—was always on the radar screen. Chickens had been roaming freely on kibbutz grounds ever since start-up days. But recognizing that there is always a ready market for fresh eggs and organically raised, free-ranging chickens, a plan of action was put into play. The seedy-looking barn once part of the long-ago Wilson ranch was rehabilitated, and a serviceable coop including five nesting cubbyholes was built inside. And *mirabile dictu*, hens started laying eggs; homemade omelets were now on Yarok's breakfast menu.

Also, beekeeping found its way onto the exploration docket: Organically produced and processed honey is always a good seller. With an eye on the future, Sophie completed a course in beekeeping offered by the community college she attended. Through conversations with classmates she learned about practicalities such as where to obtain hives and protective clothing for beekeepers. However, preliminary inquiries regarding licensing revealed that there could be a problem. County authorities held that bee stings among campers constituted a health hazard. So the project was put on hold.

A third income generator derived from animal husbandry, goat keeping, bypassed the exploration phase. Goats are hardy animals, thrive in any climate, require little attention, and make for nice pets. So in 2011 OKY purchased a pair of baby goats, a buck and a doe, belonging to the species known as Nigerian Dwarf goats. As adults, they grow to a height of 18 inches or so; and, amazingly, a doe produces an average of a quart of milk per day. In order to accommodate a starter herd—it was fondly expected that the pair of mama and papa goats would soon begin generating kids—a space for sheltering was fashioned inside the rehabbed barn. Also, a perimeter fence was put up adjacent to the barn in order to make available a grazing area for the goats.

To sum up, opportunities for generating income from agriculture and animal husbandry have been, and continue to be, explored by OKY personnel. Reaching the goal of financial independence will take effort, skill, and persistence. But in view of what has thus far been accomplished, it is by no means a futile expectation.

III. Readying Yarok for round-the-clock residency.

The third major project in OKY's plan of performance was converting Kibbutz Yarok from a summer-time to a year-round operation. This involved putting in place all the essential accommodations that would permit permanent on-site residence throughout the year.

OKY's brain trust decided to begin the process by installing minimally adequate accommodations that would make day and night residency possible during the summer season. The initial matter requiring attention was provision for overnight sleeping. It was decided that tents were the best solution. With the help of a construction crew generously made available by Camp Newman, two suitably located wood platforms were built on leveled ground. A pair of canvas tipis, each sufficiently capacious to provide sleeping space for ten or twelve avodahniks, was purchased and then erected by the construction crew. Climate control was not a concern at that moment inasmuch as the tipis were to be occupied only during the three month 'on-season', and the interiors proved to be quite comfortable even during hot afternoons. As for the cold winter months, the plan was to install heaters. These could be electrical units which received power from a feed line originating in the on-site house occupied by OKY programming staffers. Alternatively, propane-fired heating units could be used.

The next issue to be dealt with concerned disposal of human waste. OKY's planners intended to install composting toilets, which are commercially available and which are widely used in out-of-the-way locales (e.g., highway rest stops, farms and orchards, public camp grounds). Such units rely on aerobic processing to treat human excreta and, depending on the design, require little or no flush water. Operationally, bacteria which thrive at high temperatures (*ca* 120 °F.), and in the presence of oxygen, decompose the excreta into its components. Urine, very rich in plant-fortifying minerals, and other liquids can be separated out and disposed of, or collected for use in fertilizer agents.

The plan envisioned that meals would take place outdoors. There would be a cook space, and a dining area consisting of four all-in-one table-bench units, commercially available at camp supply emporia. An overhead canvas canopy equipped with detachable canvas sidewalls would make the kitchen area suitable for all-weather occupancy. However, as Robert Burns aptly phrased it: "The best laid schemes o' Mice an' Men gang aft agley..." Even before the summer of 2012 rolled around, OKY ran into a snarl of licensing problems. First off, the county authorities ruled that the pair of tipis could be used only during summer;

they would have to come down during the rest of the year. Second, the authorities deemed the compost toilets a health hazard and prohibited their installation. Third, the electricity extension lines OKY planned to run between the ranch house and the kibbutz site violated local building codes. Fourth, outdoor cooking could not be permitted because flames represented a serious fire hazard.

Given this array of impediments it was obvious that, for the time being, year-round residency was out of the question. Nevertheless, OKY decided to proceed with a summer trial run during which *in situ* experience could be useful in dealing with future contingencies. Thus, for the summer of 2012, a number of substitutive changes were developed, which would keep OKY fully in compliance with legally stipulated guidelines. Rented port-a-potties replaced compost toilets. Cooking activities would be dispensed with. No electricity would be needed for winter warmth inasmuch as the tipis were quite comfortable in summer

The summer of 2011 obviously did not go as OKY had anticipated. There was disappointment all around; among campers and their counselors, among staffers and program directors. But in view of the many obstacles, all hands cooperated in making the best of the situation. Besides, people had lots of practice in the art of improvisation. In retrospect, much had been learned that was relevant to the operational aspects of year-round residency—including the need to approach even trivial initiatives with due diligence regarding issues of licensure.

IV. Building up the 'off-season' occupancy rate.
The fourth major project on OKY's agenda focused on building up Yarok's occupancy rate during the nine-month 'off-season'. Inasmuch as the kibbutz was not able to offer visitors a residency experience, the plan was to quarter them at Camp Newman and introduce them to Kibbutz Yarok by means of tours and lectures. This would be augmented by having OKY principals lead activities for the children in the visiting groups.

The modus operandi for those heading up the project was centered on identifying groups that might be interested in visiting Newman/

Yarok, and encouraging them to do so. Mining their respective lists of contacts, which consisted mostly of groups lying within the Reform movement's orbit, highly gratifying results were produced. All told, during the nine-month 'off-season', no fewer than 15 group visits took place. Some examples:

• Congregation Beth El (Berkeley) had a weekend retreat attended by some 60 adults and children, at which an apple harvest was the central activity. OKY participated by teaching children how to bake apple crumbles, and how to make seed balls out of seeds, humus, and mud. The children then implanted them under the "Welcome to Camp Newman" banner.

• Temple Isaiah (Lafayette) had a family retreat on the weekend preceding the Hebrew month of *Iyar*. OKY staffers explained, for a group of 2nd through 7th graders, the workings of Judaism's solar-lunar calendar. They also conducted a kid-friendly version of the Jewish ceremony for welcoming a new month (the *Rosh Chodesh* ceremony).

• The Bay Area Jewish Healing Center (San Francisco) offers Jewish spiritual care to those coping with death, bereavement, or illness. It conducted a 'growing and healing' weekend at Newman. OKY participated by leading a nature exploration walk for children. This was followed by a general discussion comparing agricultural cycles (planting and harvesting) with human cycles (birth and death).

• Kehilla Community Synagogue (Oakland) selected 12 volunteers from their religious school for an overnight at Camp Newman. At 5 a.m., OKY staffers started them on a hike toward their destination. En route, kids were invited to briefly walk by themselves in the darkness. The lesson? This was how Abraham might have felt when God told him to go forth from his home [*"Lech L'cha!"*] to an unknown land.

• UC Davis Hillel (Davis) belongs to a national campus organization that serves Jewish college students. During a visit by the Davis chapter, OKY led a group of 15 guests on a tour of the kibbutz site. This was followed by a staff-led discussion about the relationship between Judaism, Zionism, and landedness. Handouts containing relevant texts taken from the Talmud were used as source materials.

Even more promising developments soon materialized. A California organization named Wilderness Torah conducts programs that seek to provide experiences illustrating how Judaism, Nature, and Spirituality interconnect with one another. Upon being contacted, they indicated their interest in using the Yarok/Newman facility as a base of operations. In particular, they mentioned group outings organized for the purpose of celebrating, in a contemporary fashion, the three traditional nature-based Jewish pilgrimage festivals of *Pesach*, *Shavu'ot*, and *Sukkot*.

Equally exciting were preliminary discussions with a national non-profit named *Chazon* (Hebrew for 'vision'). It conducts activities to promote awareness, within a Jewish context, of environmentalism. One of its programs encourages Jewish communities (e.g., congregations, JCCs, day schools) to organize a CSA—a movement that partners consumers with local family farms to their mutual benefit (Community Supported Agriculture). Informed of this, Ruben contacted *Chazon* and suggested that outings to the kibbutz by such Jewish support groups would enable them to sample a farming experience. Suffice it to say, *Chazon* expressed a serious interest.

To summarize OKY's year of 2011: How well did it succeed in meeting its proposed set of objectives? OKY had set for itself a goal of making substantive progress on four major projects: I. Vegetable production; II. Revenue streams; III. On-site residency; and IV. Occupancy rates. From all indications OKY did extremely well; and in the eyes of many, it actually outdid itself. This unquestionably redounds to the credit of all involved—directors and staffers, counselors and specialists, avodahniks and their advisors. All deserve a resonant and resounding 'well done!'

Chapter Six

INCHING TOWARD
MATURITY

*T*he summer of 2012 was characterized by a significant re-ordering in Yarok's approach to programming its activities. In the previous year a first step in this direction was taken as OKY shifted from a summer-only to a year-round operational modality. The shift got under way when the programming team, at that time Sophie Vener and Persephone Rivka, took up 12-month residency in the on-site ranch house. They revised many of the old ways of doing things, and new criteria were applied in designing and implementing a slate of activities for the ensuing summer season. But those ideas were still on the drawing boards, and none had as yet been field-tested. During the summer of 2012, avodahniks too would be resident on-site. Hence, OKY could put innovative concepts to the critical test of practical application.

As envisioned by Ruben Arquilevich, Camp Newman's Executive Director, Operation Kibbutz Yarok was charged with the design and building of a self-sustaining, cooperative, eco-friendly agrarian community. Under suitable supervision, campers would design, build, and manage the facility. When fully functional, the kibbutz would offer youngsters (and oldsters in 'off-season') an experience in Jewish communal living. The project had gotten under way in 2009, and was entering upon its fourth year.

OKY's programming team began preparing for 2012 during the run-up to the 'on-season'. The team consisted of Sophie and Persephone, plus the two associates who had recently come aboard (Angelo and Jen). First off, the team set about generating a detailed schedule of the daily routine to be followed by Yarok's resident avodahnik workforce. Once the relevant decisions came down from Camp Newman executives, OKY learned that both Newman and Yarok would be operating concurrently for a total of eight weeks starting Monday, July 16, 2012. Also, it was learned that the avodahnik selection process had yielded up a total of 64 campers who qualified for the assignment.

The first order of business was organizing the crew of avodahniks into a manageable kibbutz workforce. This complement of individuals had to be fitted into two on-site tipis, each of which could accommodate a maximum of twelve persons sleeping on floor mattresses. The OKY staff devised the following arrangement. The crew was randomly divided into eight cohorts, sorted by gender. Each cohort was accompanied by an experienced counselor known as an advisor. Because females outnumbered males by a 5:3 ratio, four cohorts consisting of ten females, and four cohorts consisting of six males, were created. Two cohorts at a time were rotated through the tipis for two-week stays. Thus, each avodahnik resided on the kibbutz for at least fourteen days. As for those six cohorts of avodahniks *not* occupying tipis at the time, they lived back at Newman, together with their advisors. Inasmuch as those teenagers were still classed as avodahniks, they worked on assignments that helped meet Newman's operational needs.

The relevant parameters having been set in place, the programming team proceeded to create a schedule of the daily weekday routine facing cohorts resident on-site at the kibbutz. The following is a synoptic summary of a day in the life of Kibbutz Yarok:

At 6:30 a.m. a shofar blast was sounded by staffer Sophie Vener, and the day got under way as the two resident cohorts roused themselves from a night of slumber. They washed up, using water pumped up from Camp Newman's wells. Two on-site rented port-a-potties, one for each gender, were available for tending to the needs of personal hygiene. The day formally commenced with the 'morning celebration'. Everyone assembled around a ring of painted rocks, and the ritual started with a sequence of breathing exercises accompanied by stylized fluid movements. The general objective was to wake up one's life forces and to propel them into active mode. Following this ritual, the group recited *T'fillah*: a group of Judaism's traditional morning prayers: *Modeh (modah) Ani, Mah Tovu Ohalechah*, plus selections from a list of prayers specifically selected for avodahnik use.

Following the morning celebration, and prior to breakfast, daily chores were tended to. There was a list of sixteen chores—e.g., sweeping out the tipis, feeding the two goats and the chickens, irrigating the plants in the greenhouse, setting up for lunch, collecting the eggs laid by chickens—that required attention. Specific chores were distributed among the avodahniks, and had to be completed before breakfast could be served. The meal was served in the on-site dining area. The kibbutz had not yet been granted a license to do open cooking because flames were deemed a fire hazard. Therefore, kitchen help delivered to Yarok the same meals as were being served at Newman for breakfast and lunch. Responsibility for clean-up after meals was rotated among teams of avodahniks. Next, the day's project assignments were distributed to the workforce. There was a morning work shift, then lunch, followed by an afternoon work shift. Work shifts were punctuated by rest breaks. Occasionally, invited guests joined the avodahniks for lunch, and afterwards favored them with a show-and-tell demonstration, or reported on a project in which the guest was involved, or engaged the avodahniks in discussing a topic of mutual interest.

The workday concluded at 4 p.m. or thereabouts. The two on-site cohorts trudged back to Newman, returning to their respective cabins. This gave them time to shower and shmooze, followed by dinner and postprandial recreational activities. The day ended for the pair of on-site cohorts as they walked back to their tipis at the kibbutz. Weary but happy, they gratefully sank into the welcoming arms of Morpheus, even before 'lights out' was signaled at 10:30 p.m.

Although the foregoing outlines the established daily routine, there were occasional departures from it. On Thursdays, the afternoon work shift was cancelled and replaced by the showing of a movie in Yarok's cinematic palace. Located in the barn, the set-up consisted of a projector, a white sheet hung against a wall in the barn, and a pair of speakers. One additional kibbutz custom deserves mention. When a pair of on-site cohorts came to the end of their two-week stay, a new pair would arrive ready to begin *their* stay. After Shabbat had come to a close on Saturday night, the departing group would build a campfire in Yarok's mud brick-glass bottle pit. The new group would then arrive and both together would observe the traditional *Havdalah* ceremony. Meanwhile, during the week, the departing group would have thought up some sort of knick-knack—a necklace or bracelet or badge—and would have made enough for presentation to the new group as a token of friendship. Then more campfire stuff, and once the festivities concluded—amid heartfelt *Shaloms* and hugs and kisses—the departing group packed up their belongings and left, while the arriving group settled into their tipis. Thus ended (and began) a pair of cohort's two week stays at Kibbutz Yarok.

—◊◊◊—

In summers past OKY's programming directors had focused most of their attention on projects designed to physically build up the kibbutz. The need to quickly get the enterprise off and running precluded paying adequate attention to a second objective: socialization of OKY's avo-dahniks. The mission statement promulgated by Camp Newman makes clear that one of its important goals is to inculcate into its campers habits of thought and patterns of behavior leading to fulfillment as a person and as a Jew. The statement, as articulated on its website, reads:

> At Camp Newman, we strive to create sacred communities of living Judaism that endow children, youth and adults with a positive Jewish identity; fostering personal growth and heightened self-esteem. . . . .We inspire campers and staff to take camp home and apply the Jewish values learned to their daily lives; ultimately bettering themselves, their communities and the world.

Inasmuch as Kibbutz Yarok is the offspring of Newman, and continues to be its ward, the scion accepts the responsibilities espoused by the sire's mission statement. Thus, OKY's goal, no less than it is Newman's, is to acquaint its avodahniks with an apperception of Judaism's beliefs, values, and practices; and to instill in them a deepened sense of Jewish identity and a love of living Jewishly.

Socialization is the process whereby youngsters acquire the knowledge, skills, and principles that enable them to participate effectively as members of a group. OKY's programming team had decided to create a roster of activities that would be informed by elements contributing to an effective socialization program. As a first step, the team developed a protocol for guiding the design of the slated activities. Searching for clues regarding the protocol's structure, the team took a close look at Camp Newman's mission statement. Scanning its wording indicated that three phrases in the statement encapsulated a trio of three different ideas relevant to socialization. Consequently, the protocol would consist of three strands.

The clause "with a positive Jewish identity" suggested that one strand should be devoted to '*Inculcating Jewishness*' into its avodahniks. In addition to teaching avodahniks about Judaism, Yarok should strive to strengthen within them a sound sense of Jewish self-identity and of allegiance to the Jewish peoplehood. The latter, incidentally, is of crucial importance in the larger scheme of things because in the final analysis survival of the Jewish peoplehood depends on generational continuity. And avodahniks are clearly members of the succeeding generation.

The mission statement's concatenated clause "fostering personal growth and heightened self-esteem" signified that a second strand ought to concern itself with advancing an avodahnik's journey towards adulthood. This socializing strand, named *'Fostering self-improvement'*, involves a willingness to undertake a guided regimen requiring self-discipline and persistence—attributes not in abundant supply among avodahniks. However, they might be willing to invest the necessary time and effort in realms that directly impact one's sense of well-being, whether physical or emotional.

The third strand in the socialization program was explicitly defined by the concluding words of Newman's mission statement: "...ultimately bettering themselves, their communities and the world." This expression clearly enunciates a Jewish concept central to much of Jewish thought and practice: *tikkun olam*. Narrowly translated, this means 'repairing the world'. However, in the course of centuries, it has come to mean: "Working to make the entire world a better place for all humankind." Named 'Actualizing *tikkun olam*', joining it with 'Inculcating Jewishness' and 'Fostering self-improvement' served to set Kibbutz Yarok's socialization agenda.

—⁓—

OKY's programming team now had in hand two of the three requisite procedural paradigms: an outline of Yarok's daily regimen, and a protocol for guiding the development of Yarok's socialization program. The third essential paradigm was drawing up a roster that would accommodate the twin goals of building up the kibbutz, and socializing the avodahniks. Turning to the first objective, activities for building up the kibbutz, the team decided to devote a sizable share of OKY's attention to the vegetable gardens inasmuch as organically grown produce was Yarok's principal crop. Accordingly, it was planned to triple the acreage devoted to vegetable garden beds. Concomitantly, it would be necessary to build additional compost piles in order to provide fertilizer for the new beds. A second planned project was the rehabilitation of a long-neglected rudimentary drip irrigation system set up years earlier. Also, fruit tree plantings would be increased substantially. Lastly, the foray into animal husbandry was proving to be promising; hence, upgrading the facility for housing the goats, and adding to the flock of chickens, was included in the roster of activities.

Regarding activities designed to advance the socialization agenda, the team chose to make use of the set of activities already fixed. But it would rely on strategies employed by perspicacious staffers for the purpose of enhancing the activity with a socializing dimension.

The OKY leadership now had in hand the three requisite instrumentalities—the daily kibbutz routine, the socialization protocol, and the activities roster—which enabled the leadership to launch the summer's program as soon as the session began. But one week into the session a hiccup developed: Persephone Rivka found it necessary to return to her family in Michigan. Disappointed but undaunted, the remaining three members of the leadership team shouldered the added burden; and, it must be added, acquitted themselves creditably throughout the entire eight-week session.

In evaluating OKY's 2012 performance, one might ask whether its achievements matched its intentions. The list of accomplishments scored by the crew of 64 avodahniks makes for a rather impressive file. Vegetable crop capacity was significantly increased by creating six new garden beds 15 feet in length, and by developing three new terraced garden beds on a sloping hillside favored with good quality soil and abundant sunshine. The rudimentary drip irrigation system was rehabilitated and also expanded. Additional compost piles were built in order to make available the necessary fertilizer for the new garden beds.

Two small groves of fruit tree saplings were planted, each grove consisting of five varietals: two apple (ripening early; ripening late), plus one each of pear, apricot, and peach. OKY staffers refined a technique known as double-digging used when implanting saplings. The technique serves to loosen compacted soil (of which the kibbutz has a surfeit) in order to expedite digging, improve irrigation, and foster root growth. Nor was the animal kingdom ignored. Chicken coop capacity was expanded by a redesign that allowed additional nesting places to be fashioned within the same limited space. Also, shade structures were built so that life would be more comfortable for Yarok's two Nigerian Dwarf goats, Reva (female) and Eitan (male).

And then there were the projects involving constructions using plain old mud. One of Yarok's invaluable building materials, this unpretentious and ungainly substance was used in two ways: bricks and plaster. The bricks were made by first fabricating wood molds of the correct shape and size. The molds were filled with mud and then sun-dried to create hardened bricks. As a plaster, mud of the desired consistency was layered as a covering over the surface of a prefabricated substrate. Over the course of the summer OKY perfected the recipe for preparing mud in the various nuanced gradations as required by end purpose. Among the objects fabricated that summer were: a bonfire pit made of mud-brick and glass bottles; a 20-foot bench constructed by applying layers of mud plaster to a sub-structure composed of recycled tires and bales of straw; and a dome-shaped, solar-heated oven six feet high and ten feet in diameter at its base.

The successes chalked up by the 2012 crew of avodahniks merited anyone's admiration. This was an assemblage of 64 volunteer teenagers, lacking previous training, who collectively put in eight weeks of work, five days per week, five hours per day. Many of these hours, it should be remembered, had to be devoted to the multitude of chores associated with maintaining the gardens: planting, weeding, watering, fertilizing, harvesting. Mindful of these considerations, how might the avodahniks' overall effort be rated? Ignoring my own biased opinion, any experienced construction manager would readily agree that this collective achievement deserved nothing less than an A+.

The goal of building up the kibbutz was incontestably met. But there was also a second goal that the programming team had resolved to pursue: socializing the crew of avodahniks. So how successful was OKY in meeting this goal? Evaluating something as nebulous as a socializing experience is a chancy endeavor. There is no way of predicting how or when a specific camp experience will show up as an affect influencing a given avodahnik's behavioral gestalt. The impact may manifest itself a week, or a year, or a decade down the road. However, data relying on surveys can provide useful information to organizations involved in socialization programs—such as Camp Newman. A well designed study assembles a large pool of representative respondents from within the targeted group. Statistical analyses then determine *averaged* responses to the survey's queries. But such surveys offer no useful information regarding any *specific* respondent's future behavior. Therefore, this approach to evaluating OKY's success in attaining its socialization goal is inapplicable in the present instance. Instead, a less than rigorous stab at an assessment of Yarok's socialization program will content itself with simply setting down a sampling of activities and events having a bearing on the process. The presentation is arranged to accord with the three-strand protocol established by Kibbutz Yarok's programming team.

• Inculcating Jewishness: Much of the material contained in Yarok's daily routine contributed to the avodahniks' store of Jewish learning. There were the traditional blessings associated with morning prayer. At meal times the cohorts recited the *motzi*. Lunch-time guest speakers also added significantly to the goal of advancing Jewish learning. One of them, for example, spoke about *shmittah*: a Jewish agricultural practice in which a field lies fallow every seventh year. Another told about a program in which participants re-enacted contemporary versions of Israel's ancient pilgrimage festivals and holidays. And a third told about an urban kibbutz that was flourishing in neighboring Berkeley.

Beyond the daily routine, some of the kibbutz buildup activities generated teaching opportunities as well. One example: creating a shaded area for the two goats led to a discussion of animal rights and the Jewish principle of *tzar b'alei chayim* ('pain felt by animals'). A second example issued from tree planting activities. This opened an opportunity to speak about Judaism's attitude towards the treatment of trees, e.g., to refrain from destroying them as a weapon in warfare. This, in turn, led to a general discussion regarding the legitimacy of scorched earth policies.

• <u>Fostering self-improvement</u>: Morning participation in yogic exercises led some avodahniks to request assistance in learning how to use yoga for the purpose of reducing stress. Still others expressed an interest in learning about meditation as a vehicle for focusing the mind. A second example is related to eating habits. Meals for breakfast and lunch, as mentioned earlier, were sent up from Newman's kitchens. So, from time to time, staffers would augment the meal with a surprise dish: a salad made from home-grown vegetables, an omelet prepared with eggs laid by the kibbutz's chickens, or a pizza baked in the on-site solar-heated oven. This provided propitious moments for discussing healthful eating and *losing weight*—a matter of no small concern to many teenagers.

In addition to the daily routine activities designed to foster self-improvement, kibbutz build-up projects also offered opportunities for doing likewise. Before building the solar-heated oven, for example, staffers asked the workforce to decide between a domed roof or flat roof; whereupon avodahniks were introduced to *consensus* decision-making as an alternative to the familiar 'majority rules' approach. In essence, the process seeks acceptance by *all* the group's members of a decision which is the first choice of *most* of them. Consensual decision-making may be a bit more cumbersome, but it is heaps more efficacious because it avoids animosities and factionalism. And needless to say, this skill can be a lifelong friend to any avodahnik.

• <u>Actualizing tikkun olam</u>: There were two situations wherein avodahniks made creditable contributions to the task of 'bettering the world for all humankind'. The first scenario originated in a *Tu B'av* celebration organized by the kibbutz staffers. It is a minor Jewish holiday dating back to biblical times and is today not widely celebrated. However, it is the only festive holiday that comes up during the summer months. Hence, OKY wisely makes the celebration part of its socialization agenda.

In biblical times the holiday featured a ritual in which prestigious families brought a free-will offering to the Temple: cords of cut up firewood for use in heating the premises. In the course of explaining the holiday, the subject of tithing in general was broached; whereupon a light bulb lit up within the avodahniks' collective cranium: Why don't *we* tithe?! Then and there, the avodahniks decided to donate one-tenth of their vegetable harvest to a food bank in nearby Santa Rosa. In my view, this is unambiguously an exemplary illustration of how a socialization gambit resulted in a tangible contribution to the holy task of *tikkun olam*.

The second scenario is similarly impressive. As previously mentioned, located on the kibbutz site is a lovely small pond; it's an ideal place for leisurely paddling about in a canoe, or for taking a bit of a dip on a hot summer afternoon. However, OKY was advised that county authorities had strictly forbidden such activities. The 'pond' was actually a dammed up section of a through waterway, which was scheduled to be restored to its original condition. Unauthorized use of the 'pond' could introduce pollutants, and would open Newman to punitive action. Kibbutzniks were dismayed, but appeals to Ruben proved unavailing. Staffers tried to mitigate the disappointment during lunchtime by recounting the Talmudic tale of Choni and the Carob Tree. In that story, an old man is asked why he is planting a carob tree which will not be bearing fruit till long after he's dead. To which Choni replied: "But someone before me planted a carob tree which I now enjoy."

The avodahniks grasped the meaning of the tale. Our lives have meaning beyond our own, and we are obliged to accept the responsibilities now for the sake of future developments, whereupon all avodahniks agreed to respect the prohibition against use of the 'pond' and to help in policing the ban. Preventing the despoilment of nature's preserve was surely a contribution to the task of 'Working to make the entire world a better place for all humankind'.

In summation, although we have only a tiny piece of evidence regarding the effectiveness of OKY's socialization effort, what we do have is certainly encouraging. There is reason to expect that the goal will be met as time marches on. And because I am addicted to seeing things through rose-colored glasses, and although I may be guilty of mistaken judgment, I nonetheless adjudge that Kibbutz Yarok has managed to make substantive progress towards meeting its socialization goals.

In concluding this chapter, I take the liberty of asserting that OKY's summer of 2012 was a pronounced success in its endeavor to build up Kibbutz Yarok and to socialize its teenagers in ways that produce individuals finding fulfillment as Jews and as human beings. And I wish all concerned—Newman and its executive director, his assistants, OKY's staffers, the avodahniks and their advisors, and sundry guests—a sincere and heartfelt *Yasher Ko'ach:* "May your strength continue to be well-directed."

An Afterword:

THE ROAD AHEAD FOR OPERATION KIBBUTZ YAROK

*R*uben Arquilevich and I have known one another since 2008. At first it was a formal relationship. He and I were the nominal heads of the two organizations, Camp Newman and the Endowment for Jewish Youth, that agreed to partner in supporting the Kibbutz Yarok project. Over the years the formal relationship has mutated into a personal friendship that strengthens with time. We appreciate one another's accomplishments, we have confidence in one another's abilities, and—no trivial matter this—we trust one another.

Every summer I make my annual visit to the kibbutz, and while at Newman, Ruben and I find time for a chat. After the hectic summer has ended and Ruben has had time to recoup a measure of sanity, he visits me at my residence in Walnut Creek. Now there is time for leisurely conversation, punctuated by buffet lunch at our favorite Indian restaurant.

Our most recent such confabulation took place in November, 2012. My agenda was headed by a concern that my estate planning attorney had brought to my attention. He had twice mentioned the advisability of making provision for the disposition of my estate. So I raise the issue with Ruben, with the understanding that we will respect confidentiality whenever it's requested.

First off, I point out that I harbor a deep affection for OKY, and I am pleased to lend it my support. But my readiness to do so hinges to an appreciable degree on his active involvement in the entire scheme of things. In the event that I become *non compos mentis*, or shuffle off this mortal coil, any directives I might have promulgated previously will possess no legal binding force—it's over. Therefore, Ruben, the unexpected and inexplicable vagaries of life being what they are, what can I do to hedge my bets?

As is invariably the case, we are entirely candid with one another. He tries to allay my first anxiety by remarking that he is perfectly content with his present *sitz im leben,* and does not even think about moving on. He follows that up by suggesting that I ought to make the acquaintance of Newman's board of directors. Although its composition may change, the board remains an entity in perpetuity. Changes in its personnel do not affect its status as an incorporated entity. Moreover, he thinks it might be prudent for me to attend the board's annual summer meeting. It takes place at Camp Newman, it's a festive weekend for the board, and attendance is very good. He'll obtain a formal invite for me to sit in and 'meet the board'. Lastly, if I'm interested, he'll share with me some of his thoughts regarding what his vision for Kibbutz Yarok foresees in the near future; say, five years down the road. Needless to say, I'm intensely interested.

Ruben prefaces his remarks by noting that Kibbutz Yarok is a unique agrarian community. It is not designed to be a permanent community housing an invariant membership. It is envisioned as an intentional community *sui generis*—literally, one of its kind. Yarok seeks to offer its temporary residents, typically urbanites, with an experience in Jewishly inflected outdoor communal living. There is no attempt to provide 'the comforts of home'. The enterprise is informed by a philosophy that seeks to redress civilization's debilitating penchant for moving humankind away from the land. The land has from aboriginal times been *Homo sapien*'s habitat; the link ought not be severed.

He begins by observing that as Kibbutz Yarok moves forward, it will strive to shape itself by respecting the parameters which extant circumstances dictate. In other words, the kibbutz will not function as a facility catering to creature comfort. Thus, Yarok will be operating in accordance with the dictates imposed by the weather pattern in the Santa Rosa mountain range, where the kibbutz is located. The annual rainy season between November and March is accompanied by frequent storms and cold spells. For the kibbutz this means that the tipis are uninhabitable, and that the dirt road connecting to Camp Newman becomes a virtually impassable quagmire. Rectifying the situation would mean departing from the basic premise of 'getting back to nature'. Paving the road would entail a totally unjustifiable expenditure, and would represent a concession to the regrettable prevailing ideology of covering the planet with concrete. For the tipis, making them habitable year-round would mean investing in a substantial amount of infrastructure. This sort of undertaking requires surmounting a goodly number of hurdles set in place by county and environmental authorities who are in no way adversarial; rather, it is their responsibility to protect the citizenry's common good. He has much experience, he tells me, in jockeying back and forth with such agencies on behalf of Camp Newman. So unless the need is imperative, it is a daunting process that OKY will stay away from. As Ruben foresees it, OKY will be, and will remain, an eight-month operation running from March to November.

Next item on his agenda is the matter of size in terms of kibbutz inhabitants. He believes that Yarok should settle in at something in the neighborhood of 40 people. He thinks that number comprises a viable community, while preserving the necessary intimacy. This will require constructing two additional tipis, each able to house a dozen or so persons sleeping on bunk mattresses. Also, dining facilities will need upgrading in order to accommodate taking breakfast and lunch on-site. Dinner, as it is at present, will be taken in a sequestered wing of Camp Newman's dining hall. Showering and recreational activities utilizing its facilities will also be done at Newman. This arrangement, I venture to interject, will entail making a one-mile hike down to Newman, and another hike back up to Yarok for sleeping. This will necessarily limit enrollment to individuals able and willing to rough it. Indeed it will, he responds. Want to experience outdoor living? Well, this is it!

Leadership is another matter in need of restructuring. Ruben has already set things in motion by making arrangements for 2013. Conversations are being conducted with candidates for the position of year-round resident Farm Manager. The intention is to have the person selected live year-round in part of the ranch house. The rest of the house will be reserved for studios in which that summer's crew of avodahniks can pursue programmed projects. As an adjunct to the leadership team, a Program Director will be appointed who will serve OKY full-time during the summer of 2013, and part-time in the 'off-season'.

With regard to long-term leadership, Ruben considers it essential that a working partnership be established with an organization having expertise in outdoor living activities—an expertise neither Newman nor Yarok possesses. To this end, a collaboration that seems to augur well for the future has already been initiated. Founded in 2007, Wilderness Torah celebrates the earth-based traditions of Judaism to nourish the connections between self, community, earth, and spirituality. Its operations are centered in the Bay Area, and its programming includes an annual cycle of group outings for the purpose of celebrating, in contemporary fashion, the three traditional nature-based Jewish pilgrimage festivals (*Pesach, Shavu'ot,* and *Sukkot*). Wilderness Torah made use of the Yarok/Newman facility as a base of operations for the *Pesach* group outing. Things went very well and both parties are satisfied with the results of the collaborative initiative. Ruben considers creation of a formal partnership in the not-too-distant future a distinct possibility.

Another partnership, while limited in its prospective benefits, is nevertheless worth maintaining and even strengthening: Kibbutz Lotan. Alex Ciselsky, one of its founders, is a good friend of Ruben, and they interact often in regard to matters of personnel. He advises Ruben about qualified summer counselors and specialists for Newman and Yarok.

Ruben, in turn, recommends Lotan to campers who inquire about places in which to learn about permaculture and associated ecological subjects as part of an Israeli experience. Besides, Alex is well-connected and a general good-will ambassador.

The preceding concerns itself with Ruben's long-term objectives. And what are his thoughts regarding the short term; say the summer of 2013? He certainly expects OKY to give assiduous attention to expanding the vegetable crop. This effort has proven to be the closest thing yet to an income generator for the kibbutz. In addition to vegetables, growing organic herbs ought to be considered as a candidate for producing a revenue stream. Also quite promising is the potential inherent in fruit tree cultivation. Aside from the fruit itself, trees bring Yarok many benefits. They anchor the soil, aid in water retention, serve as windbreaks, furnish composting detritus, and provide welcome shade on hot summer days. Speaking of shade, Ruben mentions his plan to build rest areas in two shady spots at the opposite sides of the pond—a place of respite after a work shift on a sweltering mid-summer day. Furthermore, the pond, small as it may be, could nevertheless be developed into a venue for recreational activity. Cleaned up, and with a credentialed lifeguard on duty, it could be used for both swimming, and for leisurely paddling about in clunky would-be canoes. (A real canoe could zip across the pond in three seconds flat.)

On the subject of trees, Ruben returns to his idea of cultivating a modest-sized citron grove. A citron (*etrog* in Hebrew) is one of the species used as a ritual object in celebrating the Jewish holiday of Sukkot. What a boon that would be for little Kibbutz Yarok. Every one of the Reform movement's 700+ congregations is a prospective purchaser of an oky-doky etrog! Besides, think of the renown it garners for Camp Newman! I can see that he's serious about this possibility; he plans to follow up by contacting some of his acquaintances in southern California, his erstwhile stomping ground.

He doesn't foresee much activity in the realm of animal husbandry. Certainly the chicken flock deserves expansion; chickens practically care for themselves. But adding livestock may be a bit too ambitious; they are susceptible to infection, and veterinarians are mighty expensive... But, he adds, we might perhaps add a llama or two; they're hardy and get along well with goats. Beekeeping? The likelihood of bee stings makes that a mite risky.

So, I've exhausted the list of questions I had prepared for Ruben, which he has answered fully. Moreover, he has supplemented them with additional important information. Now it's time for lunch, so we head for our favorite Indian restaurant and its delectable buffet menu. He knows the route to Sargam, so he drives. Our leisurely repast over, I'm driven back to my residence, and we exchange warm *Shaloms* to conclude the visit. As usual, it's been an exceedingly pleasant experience. I'll be seeing him once again, on his turf, come this summer.

Appendix A:
A Summary of Permaculture
Theory and Practice

*T*he name 'permaculture' is a coinage that appeared in the 1970s and is a conflation of 'permanent' and 'agriculture'. The movement concerns itself with the design and maintenance of sustainable land use systems. Based on ecological principles, permaculture's ideas can hopefully assist communities in establishing functional, self-sustaining communities that meet their members' food, energy, shelter, material, and non-material needs. In the discussion that follows, a large body of material has been condensed into more manageable proportions.

I. **Ethical Principles**

Permaculture advocates adherence to three ethical principles couched in the form of a motto: *Earthcare, Peoplecare, Fairshare.* These three core values inform every aspect of the movement's theory and practice. If stakeholders commit to permacultural practice, they are urged to commit as well to the ethical principles.

Earthcare: This planet is the source of all life; human beings are its custodians, not its masters. We are enjoined from despoiling or ravaging it. Permaculture supports all initiatives that seek to promote mutually beneficial relationships among the elements comprising the Earth's vast ecological system. Permaculture's objective is to develop land-use strategies that create an alliance between people and the environmental factors indispensable to their survival.

Peoplecare: At the local level, a permaculture community owes its members, the ill and the aged included, the wherewithal for meeting their basic needs adequately in an environment that frees them from financial worries. On the universal level, permaculture enjoins people everywhere to allot and distribute the Earth's limited resources in ways that are morally equitable, respect human dignity, and injure neither the planet nor its inhabitants.

Fairshare: The term 'fairshare' implies a willingness to dispense justice to everyone in all walks of life. *Social justice*: the absence of discrimination based on distinctions related to class, gender, ethnicity, sexuality, or religion. *Economic justice*: equality of opportunity commensurate with ability, and the absence of exploitation by the strong of the weak. *Legal justice*: the absence of oppressive restrictions imposed by authoritative institutions on one's licit way of life or patterns of behavior.

II. **Design Principles**

Functionally, two main principles serve as guidelines in designing a permaculture community. One is to analyze nature's eco-systems and to pattern the community's activities after such aspects of nature's designs as are usefully applicable. The second design principle pertains to the elements that comprise the total system and, most importantly, how these elements are interconnected so that outputs of one become the inputs to another.

Emulating nature's eco-systems: Nature's eco-systems have evolved over eons of time. As such, these systems are the result of endless experimentation, modification, and winnowing. Consequently, permaculture design takes note of patterns that exist in nature, observes how they function, and assesses their potential for being usefully adapted to the landscape at hand. An example of nature's wisdom: Natural forests do not consist exclusively of tall trees. Nature seeks to maximize the conversion of impinging solar energy into plant growth by capturing light that has filtered through the trees. Therefore, it employs a stratagem called 'layering': encouraging the growth of plant species of successively shorter physical heights. Another example: The interface between a pond and its shoreline is not a neat circle, but tends to be irregularly curvaceous. The reason is that an irregular boundary, with its ins and outs, increases the amount of edge for a given area. Hence, productivity is higher. The foregoing examples illustrate how designers of permaculture land use systems can add to the tools of their trade by imitating nature's strategies.

Optimizing synergistic linkups: A system is defined as a set of connected elements forming a complex whole. A permaculture community is such a system. If the elements are linked together whereby the output of one becomes the input to another, the coupling can produce a combined effect exceeding the sum of the two separate effects. In other words, synergy is at work. Sound permaculture design seeks to connect systemic elements together with a prolific network of linkages. The richer the network, the higher the system's efficiency because waste is minimized, labor requirements are reduced, energy is conserved, and there is lesser dependence on non-renewable resources. All these savings can be looked upon as incomes when examining the community's balance sheet. And needless to say, a permaculture enterprise cannot long endure if it ignores the 'bottom line'.

III. Operational Principles

A permaculture community is a dynamic entity and encounters inevitable change. Some changes are unanticipated and variegated—weather, 'acts of god', human error, random perturbations, pure mischance. They must be dealt with on an *ad hoc* basis. However, *planned* changes can be introduced in accordance with principles that optimize the operation. One of these refers to the entity's rate of growth, and the second refers to the entity's cash crops.

Favoring gradualism: Permaculture favors a policy of gradual growth: starting on a small scale and building stepwise on success. The movement lives quite comfortably with the aphorism popularized in the 1970s ('Small is beautiful') because a system following a strategy of slow growth is easier to maintain, is easier to set aright in case of miscalculation, and in the long run produces consistently positive outcomes.

A policy of gradualism is especially important during a permaculture community's formative period. Creation of such a community is an emotion-packed event, and the tendency is to rush ahead. But haste makes waste. Gradualism is a good way not only to avoid crippling catastrophe, but it also helps forestall the negative fallout associated with fault-finding and back-biting—an inevitable consequence of setbacks resulting from unjustifiably hurried deeds. In sum, permaculture prefers gradual change rather than impetuous leaps.

Supporting polyculture: In agrarian systems, polyculture means growing different types of crops within a given tract of arable land. Permaculture advocates a policy of polyculture, as opposed to monoculture. While conceding that monoculture is the more profitable strategy—a single crop is easier to plant, maintain, and harvest—permaculture supports the polyculture option for a number of cogent reasons. First, biodiversity is a hedge against crop failure due to disease. Arrival of a pathogenic vector that's inimical to a given crop spells total disaster if it alights upon a monocultural stand of said crop. In the case of polycultural diversity, only the targeted crop takes a hit; the others survive unscathed.

Second, aware of the danger that disease poses in monoculture, managers hedge their bets by using copious quantities of chemical pesticides. Needless to say, such measures produce comestibles that are harmful to humans. And even when used as feedstock for animals, there is injury to soil and water resources, as well as indirectly to humans. And third, biodiversity makes for soil able to provide habitat for a great variety of organisms. Some of these will turn out to be species that aid cross-pollination, or enhance fertilization, or contribute to biological types of pest control.

Appendix B:
Cosmology, Tikkun Olam, and
the Lurianic Scenario

*I*n the aftermath of the calamitous events in Spain that had driven the Jews into exile, a coterie of kabbalists in Palestine had coalesced into an amorphous community located in the holy city of Safed and its environs. The loose-knit community was centered on the charismatic Rabbi Yitz'chak Luria, likewise a refugee from Spain.

The community, still traumatized by recent events, was wrestling with the age-old problem of divine justice: Why does God—perfect in every way—permit innocents to suffer? In pondering this enigma, Rabbi Luria and his coterie of acolytes developed a cosmological scenario that described how the material world came into being.

In kabbalistic discourse, God is usually referred to as *Ein Sof*—the One Without End in both time and space. According to the Lurianic scenario, at some point in primordial time God decided to create a perfect universe. But the task was prodigious and so *Ein Sof*, after willing the universe's creation, decided to simplify the task by calling upon the assistance of ten intermediaries (the ten *S'firot*). But inasmuch as God filled all space, *Ein Sof* deliberately withdrew its substance from part of its infinite domain in order to make room for the ten *S'firot*. Whereupon ten empty vessels, capable of interacting with one another, were created.

Next, *Ein Sof* projected an intense ray of divine light into each empty vessel. However, the light was so intense that not all the vessels could withstand its tremendous pressure. Of the ten, three remained intact, six were slightly impaired, and the tenth was seriously damaged. The *S'firot* hastily mustered their forces and set to work repairing things. All was quickly set aright—all, except for the tenth vessel. The damage was so severe that despite the collective efforts of the other nine vessels, only a partial, rather than a complete, restoration could be effected. This specific *S'firah* happened to be an important element in the cosmological scheme of things because it, and it alone, was responsible for creating and sustaining the material world. Consequently, although the world was created as planned, it was a flawed world. And for the material world to be perfected it was necessary for its inhabitants to participate in the mending process by doing good works (*i.e.,* performing mitzvot). Failing this, the final restoration would remain incomplete.

—〜—

The Lurianic model brilliantly introduced three radically new elements into the cosmic creation story, each furnishing an insight into the way the divine and the human articulate together. First, exile—something about which Rabbi Luria and his circle had painful direct knowledge—is part of the divine order of things. Whether voluntary or imposed, comprehensible or perplexing, celestial or earthly, the act of exile needs to be accepted as an existing verity. Second, the workings of *Ein Sof*, as well as of *Homo sapiens*, don't always proceed according to plan. A miscalculation—here or there, large or small, intuited or anticipated—and the entire venture can suddenly shatter and go to pieces. And third, human beings have a non-negotiable obligation to participate in the task of repairing the world. In a Jewish context, this precept devolves into the task of contributing to the work of *Tikkun Olam*. Unless Jews, through mitzvot, send up the holy sparks needed to rehabilitate the tenth *S'firah*, the goal of a perfected world cannot be attained. In short, the Jewish peoplehood is now partnered with the divine in striving to arrive at the messianic era.

Appendix C:
An Avodahnik's Essay

*C*laire Kotarski; September, 2012.

Holiness is found in a quarter bucket of straw, half a bucket of sand, a whole bucket of earth, and as much water as needed in order to get that smooth texture: the recipe to create the perfect mud. This summer, with 63 of my new best friends, some of whom are here this weekend, I got the chance to experience my Avodah summer at Camp Newman. That mud was created by us, and molded into a bench, fire pit, and oven to cook our own pizza. About a mile away from main camp lies Operation Kibbutz Yarok (OKY for short), a part of the camp property that practices and teaches sustainable agriculture and all things awesome. I was given the chance to live there for 2 weeks. I rose only from the sound of the shofar and the rays of light that flooded through our tipi door. We would circle together before breakfast to stretch, meditate, and say "hello" to the sun. I fell in love with this land. Here I was given the opportunity to shape it, watch it evolve, and witness it as something living. It took our guidance, and it gave it back to us: all of us working for our fair share. I learned so much more in the outdoor environment, and felt so much more inspired. The camp food tasted better with the sounds of chickens roaming and a pinch of sea salt. I did the things I had promised myself I would do when I had more free time during the year. I got things done, and saw the product of my effort. I realized how much it takes to truly feed oneself, and provide for a community. These strangers I met on the first day soon came to be the people I would go to for advice and wisdom. Our bonds grew closer because we were taken out of our element, back to the land.

This place is hard to put into words, and I apologize if what I described is tough to visualize. The smells and sounds of OKY resonate so well in my mind. It brings me comfort to go back to the place when I need to, and I am so fortunate for my memories. However, with time, these feelings can fade. I am still trying to figure out how to incorporate what I have learned and my heightened sense of spirituality into my daily life. OKY has provided me with the holiness of generosity. I learned that you can be independent, but not be afraid to ask for help. I am determined to heal the world with happy glances, and see the beauty in everything. At one point in the summer during *t' fillah*, we formed an inner and outer circle facing each other. We went around calling ourselves to prayer with the *Barchu*, holding the hands of the person in front of us and staring at them straight in the eyes. What started as an exercise of discomfort and sweaty hands led to an appreciation of the person in front of me. I actually took time to look. With the light of the fire, I felt extremely human.

Living in Los Angeles, at the heart of the city, it can be challenging to find what calms me. Earth, wind, water, and fire are hard to come by. There are imbalances. Sophie Vener, the specialist at the Kibbutz, told me that she sits at her garden when she feels frustration. She imagines how the plants grow, and how she cared for them, and how they are taking nutrients from our Earth. Now, while walking in the halls at school, I notice the tree outside my classroom window. I don't mind if a fly is in the house. Because these are the holy moments I have missed since August, calling me back to the land I love.

A List of Bibliographical References

Steinberg, Milton, *Basic Judaism*, New York: HJB Publishers, 1947.
An excellent, unbiased, and accessible introduction to the subject.

Oliner, Samuel, *Do Unto Others*, Boulder, CO: Westview Press, 2003.
The extraordinary acts of ordinary people which exemplify the
essence of tikkun olam.

Meyer, Michael, *Response to Modernity*, New York: Oxford University
Press, 1988. A thoroughly researched history of the Reform movement in the United States. Note: Does not go beyond the early 1980s.

Miles, William, *Zion in the Desert*, Albany, NY: State University of
New York Press, 2007. An engaging treatment of life in the Reform
movement's two kibbutzim in Israel.

Sales, Amy, and Leonard Saxe, *How Goodly Are Thy Tents*, Lebanon,
NH: University Press of New England, 2004.
A well-documented survey of summer camps as Jewish social-
izing experiences.

Dimont, Max, *Jews, God and History*, New York: Simon and Schuster,
1962. A very concise, but thoroughly readable, account of three
millennia of Jewish history that successfully captures the critical
nodal points of the journey.

Donin, Hayim, *To Pray as a Jew*, New York: Basic Books, 1980.
A detailed guide to the prayer book and the synagogue service
written from an Orthodox point of view.

Lorge, Michael, and Gary Zola (eds.), *A Place of Our Own*, Tuscaloosa, AL: University of Alabama Press, 2006. A collection of essays describing the early history of Reform camping in the U.S.

Klein, Isaac, *A Guide to Jewish Religious Practice*, New York: The Jewish Theological Seminary of America, 1979. A compendium, written from a Conservative perspective, dealing with halachic principles as they pertain to Jewish life.

Hemenway, Toby, *Gaia's Garden* (2nd ed.), White River Junction, VT: Chelsea Green Publishing, 2009. Provides a wide-ranging look at permaculture's history, theory, and practice.

Index

Page locators in *italics* indicate photographs.

Abrams, Martin, 23, *34*
Academy for Jewish Religion, 15–16
"Actualizing *tikkun olam*," 82, 86–87
American Jewish University, 54
American Reform Judaism, 57
Arquilevich, Ruben
    camp management career, 54–57
    and Colorado College, 54
    and creation of OKY, 21–22, 55–57, 59–60
    OKY dedicatory celebration, 2, 4, 6, 8, 9, 11, *35*, 48
    OKY first year evaluation, 60–62
    OKY off-season programs, 75
    OKY year-round staff and operations, 62–64, 77–78
    planning for future of OKY, 89–94
    visiting kibbutzim during childhood, 53–54
avodah (work and service), 4
avodahniks
    activities roster, 82–84

an avodahnik's essay, 103–4
daily routine and work schedule, 78–80
OKY dedicatory celebration, 4, 5, *37*, *38*, 60–61
OKY vegetable garden, 3–4, *37*, 61, 67–69
socialization, 80–82, 85–88

barn and live animal farm, 3, *30*, *31*
bashert (destined), 64
Bay Area Jewish Healing Center, 74
Bay Area traffic, 1–2, 11
beekeeping, 71
berries, 70
birkat ha-mazon (traditional Shabbat meal blessing), 10
bonfire pit, 80, 84
bunkhouse construction, 3, 4–6, *36*, 60–62

Camp Cejwin, 42–43
Camp Cobbossee, 42
Camp Kutz, 63
camp management, 54–57
Camp Modin, 43
Camp Newman
    Camp Saratoga/Camp Swig, 45–47, 48–51
    and creation of OKY, *ix–x*, 21–22, 55–57
    entrance portal, *27*
    founding of, 47–49, 55
    growth of, 51–52
    and Jewish summer camps in the U.S., 41–45
    long-range objectives, 2
    mission statement, 80–81
    and planning for future of OKY, 90–93
    and Union for Reform Judaism (URJ), 50
    and Union of American Hebrew Congregations (UAHC), 43–44, 45–49

Camp Olin-Sang-Ruby Union Institute (OSRUI), 44

Camp Saratoga, 45–46

Camp Shalom, 55

Camp Swig, 46–47, 48–51, 55

Camp Swig-Newman, 48, 50–51

Camp Tawonga, 67

camping, Jewish traditions of, 41–43

canoeing on the pond, *38*, 87, 93

Central Jewish Institute (CJI), 42–43

Chazon (vision) nonprofit, 75

chickens, 70, 84, 93–94

Choni and the Carob Tree, 87

Ciselsky, Alex, 92

City College of New York, 14

Cohen, Michael M., 20, 23, *34*

Colorado College, 54

Community Supported Agriculture (CSA), 75

compost, 68, 83

composting toilets, 72, 73

compromise, spirit of compromise, 6

Congregation Beth El, 74

Congregation Emanu-el, 45

Congregation Shir Neshamah, 16

consensual decision-making, 86

cosmology and *tikkun olam*, 99–101

cover crops, 68

crop yield improvements, 67–69

design principles of permaculture, 96–97

Earthcare, Peoplecare, Fairshare, 95–96

eggs, 70

Ein Sof (the One Without End), 99–100

Eisendrath, Rabbi Maurice, 43–44
emulation of nature's eco-systems, 96–97
Endowment for Jewish Youth (EJY)
    and Birthright Israel trips, 18–19
    board members, 23
    creation of, 17–18
    financial support for Kibbutz Yarok, 2–3, 21–23, 56–57
    and Jewish day schools, 18
    Jewish summer camps and camp scholarships, 19–21
    mission statement, 18
ethical principles of permaculture, 95–96
etrog (citron), 93

"for profit" camps, 42–43
foreword, *ix–x*
"Fostering self-improvement," 82, 86
Foundation for Jewish Camp, 19–20
"fresh air" camps, 41–42
Freund, Rabbi Iser, 45
fruit trees, 70, 83–84, 93

Glass, Joe, *x*, 65–66, 67
goats and goat milk, 71, 84, 85–86
gradualism, 97–98
greenhouse construction, 69
Groesberg, Rabbi Sholom
    decision to enter rabbinate, 13, 15–16
    and Endowment for Jewish Youth (EJY), 17–23, *34*
    engineering career, 14–15
    estate planning, 16–17, 89–90
    financial support for OKY, 89–90
    parents and childhood, 13–14

Grossberg, Henry, 23
Gwasdoff, Rabbi Jason, 6, *36*

HaRo'ah HaK'tanah (Israeli folk dance), 11
Havdalah ceremony, 80
Hebrew Union College (HUC), 44–45
herbs, 70, 93
Herzl, Theodor, 64
Holy *Shechinah* (divine Presence), 8
honey, 71

Im tirtzu, ein zo aggadah (If you will it, it is no dream), 64
"Inculcating Jewishness," 81–82, 85–86
Israel Movement for Progressive Judaism (IMPJ), 57–58
Israeli kibbutzim, 53–54, 57–60

Jewish Agency (JA), 58
Jewish Community Center (JCC) camps, 48
Jewish summer camps in the U.S. (historical), 41–43
Judaism, positive Jewish identity (socialization of avodahniks), 80–82, 85–88
jweekly (newspaper), 3

kashrut (kosher dietary laws), 59
Katzki, Dan, 3, 8
Katzki, Lisa
    and creation of OKY, 21–22, 23
    and Endowment for Jewish Youth (EJY), 17, *34*
    OKY dedicatory celebration, *x*, 2, 3, 7, 8
Kaufman, Dena, 2
Kehilla Community Synagogue, 74
Kibbutz Lotan, 57, 59–60, 63, 92–93
Kibbutz Yahel, 57, 58–59

Kibbutz Yarok. *See* Operation Kibbutz Yarok (OKY)

Kotarski, Claire, 103–4

kvelling (silently bursting with pride), 3

Lebow, Cheryl, 23, *34*

Levine, Rabbi Raphael, 44

live animal farm, 3, *30*, *31*, 70–71

Los Angeles JCC, 55

Luria, Rabbi Yitz'chak, 99

Lurianic model of *tikkun olam*, 99–101

Ma'or, Ido, 60

Mezuzah on bunkhouse doorway, 5–6, *36*

mulching, 68

National Federation of Temple Youth (NFTY), 44

nature

    Anne Frank on the solace of nature, *v*

    emulation of nature's eco-systems, 96–97

Negev Desert, 58–59

Newman, Raquel, 47–48

Norris, Kathleen Thompson, 45

Operation Kibbutz Yarok (OKY)

    aerial view, *26*

    avodahniks' activities roster, 82–84

    avodahniks' daily routine and work schedule, *29*, 78–80

    avodahniks' socialization, 80–82, 85–88

    barn and live animal farm, 3, *30*, *31*

    bunkhouse construction, 3, 4–6, *36*, 60–62

    canoeing on the pond, *38*

    creation of, 21–22, 55–57, 59–60

    dedicatory celebration, 1, 2, 4–9, 11, *35*, *36*, 48

design and beginning of, 1–3
dining hall, 9–10
entrance to, *28*
experience of nature and working the land, *ix–x*
first year evaluation, 60–62
key staff, 2
meds time for campers, 9–10
off-season programs, 73–75
on-season program planning, 65–66
planning for future of, 89–93
prayer bench construction, *39*
revenue stream expansion, 69–71
security at, 2
Shabbat dinners at, 4, 10–11
Shabbat services at, 8–9, 11, 80
vegetable garden, 3–4, 10, *37*, 60–62, 67–69, 82–83, 93
year-round programming, 77–78, 91–94
year-round residency preparations, 71–73
year-round staff and operations, 62–64, 66–67
operational principles of permaculture, 97–98
organic gardening revenue streams, 70–71
Orthodox Judaism, 57
oven construction, 84, 86

Pacific Association of Reform Rabbis, 45
Pazornik, Amanda, 3, 4
permaculture, 63, 95–98
philanthropic giving, 20–21
Poalei Tziyon (Workers of Zion) movement, 13
polyculture, 98
pond at OKY, *38*, 87, 93
positive Jewish identity (socialization of avodahniks), 80–82, 85–88
prayer bench construction, *39*, 84

Progressive Judaism, 58–59
See also Reform Judaism
P.S. 100, 14

Recht, Rick, 9
Reform Judaism
    and Israel Movement for Progressive Judaism (IMPJ), 57–58
    and Israeli kibbutzim, 57–59
    and off-season OKY programs, 73–75
    Union for Reform Judaism (URJ), 50, 56, 63
Reichenbach, Paul, 56
Rembrandt Venture Partners, 49
Rivka, Persephone, 63–64, 65–66, 67, 77, 78, 83
Roselin, Lillian, 22, 23, 34
Rosh Chodesh (new month) ceremony, 74
ru'ach (spiritedness), 51
Ruhman, Shelley, 3, 8

S-generation, 10
sabra (Israeli-born) Jews, 58
Schindler, Rabbi Alexander, 47
Shabbat dinners at OKY, 4, 10–11
Shabbat services at OKY, 8–9, 11, 80
Shalom uv'rachah! (May you be granted peace and blessing), 52
Shehecheyanu prayer, 6
Shone Farm, 66
Silva, Angelo, 66–67, 70, 78
Singer, Allen, 2, 3, 7, 8, 23, 34
Smith, Rabbi Allan, 46, 55
socialization of avodahniks, 80–82, 85–88
soil quality improvements, 67–69
solar-heated oven, 84, 86
Stevens Institute of Technology, 14
Swanson, Jen, 67, 78

Swig, Benjamin H., 46
synergistic linkup optimization, 97

Temple de Hirsch, 45
Temple Isaiah, 74
Temple Israel, 6
the ten *S'firot* (intermediaries), 99–101
T'fillah (morning prayers), 79
tikkun olam (repairing the world), 82, 86–87, 99–101
tipis at OKY, 72–73, 78–80, 91, 103
Todah rabbah (many, many thanks), 5, 23
Tu B'av celebration, 86–87

UAHC Youth Division, 46–47, 51, 55, 58
UC Davis Hillel, 74
Union for Reform Judaism (URJ), 50, 56, 63
Union of American Hebrew Congregations (UAHC), 43–44, 45–49
University of Judaism (American Jewish University), 54

Vared, Ari, *x*, 2, 10, 59, 60, 65
vegetable garden, 3–4, 10, *37*, 60–62, 67–69, 82–83, 93
Vener, Sophie, 62–64, 65–66, 67, 68, 71, 77, 78, 79
volunteers at OKY, 66–67

Widener University, 14–15
Wilderness Torah, 75, 92
Wilson Ranch, 56, 70

yarok (green), 3
Yasher Ko'ach (May your strength continue to be well-directed), 88
year-round residency preparations, OKY, 71–73
Yoffie, Rabbi Eric, 47
yoga, 86